Reflections

To Be a Pilgrim

Further Reflections on the Psalms of Ascents

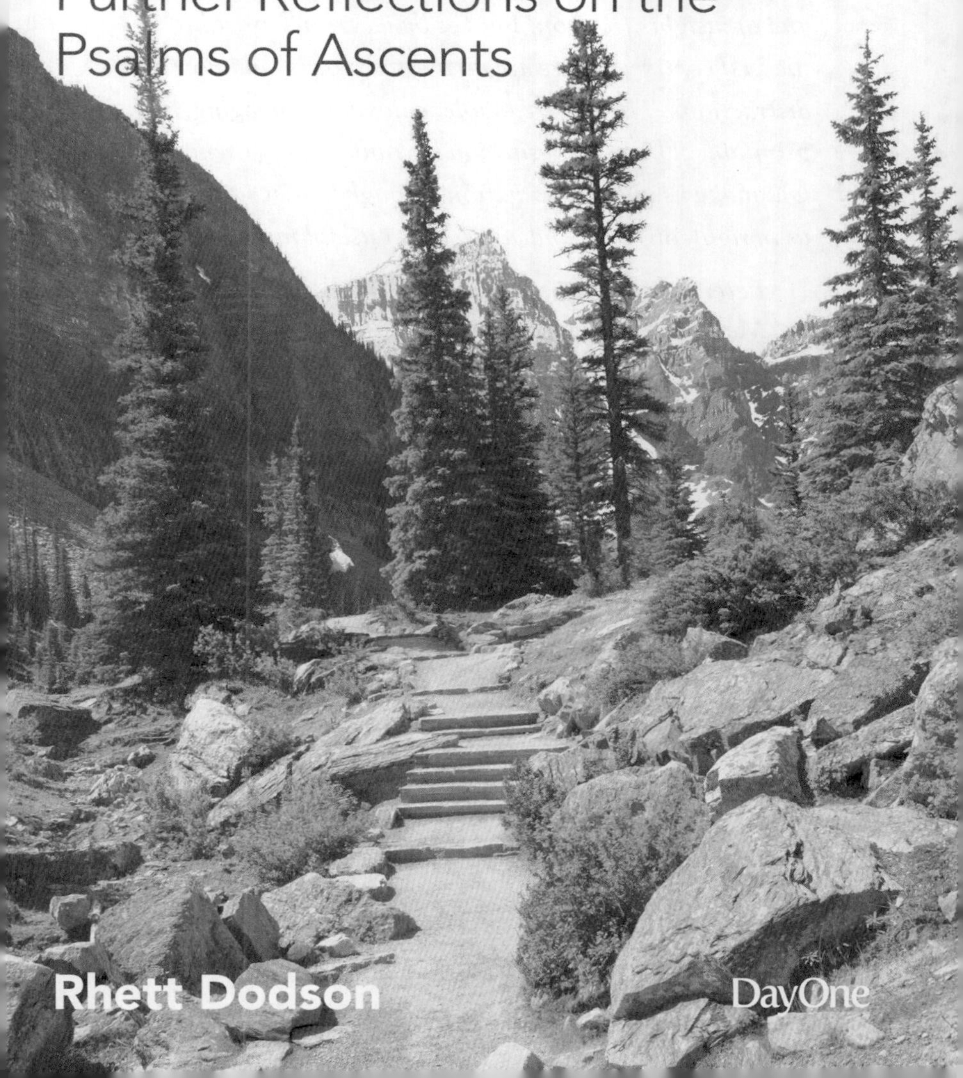

Rhett Dodson

DayOne

Endorsements

These expositions by Rhett Dodson are a model for us all, lay people and ministers alike. The exposition of each psalm is true to the text and true to our life in God today. Each one makes good use of the content and structure of the psalm, of insights from the Old and New Testaments, and of insights from our lives as believers in Christ in the 21st century. There are no wasted words, and no distractions. They are readable, enjoyable, engaging, and profitable. I have no hesitation in commending them. They will make us wise for salvation through Christ Jesus, train us in righteousness, and equip us for useful ministry.

Peter Adam, former Principal, Ridley College, Melbourne, Australia, and author of Speaking God's Words

The Psalms of Ascents still throb with the ancient excitement of a people going to meet their God in worship. Rhett Dodson writes with the heart of a pastor as well as the background of a scholar. His devout treatment of these psalms reminds us that they were written for us as well as for the generations of Israelites who first sang them.

Peter Lewis, Senior Pastor, Cornerstone Evangelical Church, Nottingham, UK, and author of The Genius of Puritanism ***and*** The Glory of Christ

This is a great read of unusual quality for its clarity, shrewd insights, and practical, pastoral stimulus. Each psalm is treated as an entity, with the Bible text always clearly in the driving-seat. Yet each is also related to the whole sweep of biblical theology and especially to the centrality of our Lord Jesus Christ. The contemporary applications are down-to-earth and realistic, as well as challenging and motivational, heart-warming, and spirit-uplifting. This is the best sort of expository Bible teaching, which I commend both very warmly and very gratefully for the blessing it has been to me.

David Jackman, past President of the Proclamation Trust, London, UK, and author of Teaching Isaiah

In a day when expositions can polarize into either very dry bread or very mushy bread, here is a fine feast. In this book and its companion volume, Rhett Dodson expounds the wonderful "Psalms of Ascents" (Psalms 120–134) with attention to the text and its message (how much we need this!), illustrations drawn from rich wells, familiarity with the normal Christian life, and readability that befits a good communicator. I found myself grateful again to God for these psalms and for someone to steer me through their meaning and applications. You will assent as well, I am sure!

Simon Manchester, Senior Minister, St. Thomas Anglican Church, North Sydney, Australia, and author of Six Steps to Talking about Jesus

The collection of psalms known as the Songs of Ascents is not the easiest to exegete and apply, but Rhett Dodson has opened up these ancient songs for modern readers and applied them to a variety of life situations in a compelling and attractive way. Readers of these expositions will find themselves drawn into an old world of pilgrims journeying to worship—and will also find themselves, in the variety of their life's experiences, drawn to worship with them. I am sure that all who know the God of Zion, and who confess themselves to be pilgrims and strangers on the earth, will find in these studies words of encouragement and strength for the journey.

Iain D. Campbell, Minister, Point Free Church of Scotland, Isle of Lewis, UK, and author of On the First Day of the Week ***and*** Heroes and Heretics

The Psalms of Ascents are a great source of pastoral applicability, and this book will encourage us to read the psalms and enjoy them!

Josh Moody, Senior Pastor, College Church, Wheaton, IL, USA, and author of No Other Gospel

British Library Cataloguing in Publication Data available

ISBN 978-1-84625-355-3

Published by Day One Publications
Ryelands Road, Leominster, HR6 8NZ

☎ 01568 613 740
FAX: 01568 611 473
email—sales@dayone.co.uk
web site—www.dayone.co.uk
North American e-mail—usasales@dayone.co.uk
North American web site—www.dayonebookstore.com

Designed by Wayne McMaster and printed by Orchard Press Cheltenham Ltd

To my mother, Lucy Dodson,
who has always wanted me to write

Companion volume

This Brief Journey:

Loving and Living the Psalms of Ascents

ISBN 978-1-84625-354-6

Contents

Introduction 10

1 *Your blessed life now* 12

2 *God's victory over evil* 26

3 *Out of the depths* 40

4 *Stressed!* 54

5 *Seeking God's presence* 72

6 *Experiencing God's presence* 86

7 *The beauty of unity* 100

8 *Blessing given and received* 112

Endnotes 124

Introduction

This volume continues the studies begun in *This Brief Journey: Loving and Living the Psalms of Ascents* and covers Psalms 128–134. The Israelites used this collection of psalms for their journeys to Jerusalem for the three annual pilgrim feasts: Unleavened Bread (Passover), Weeks (Pentecost), and Booths (Tabernacles) (Exod. 23:14–17; Deut. 16:16). These psalms instruct, inspire, and guide every pilgrim headed to Jerusalem, the believer's heavenly home.

As with the previous volume, the chapters of this book began as a series of expositions delivered in Calgary, Alberta, and were later restudied, reworked, and preached to my congregation, Grace Presbyterian Church (PCA) in Hudson, Ohio. I am grateful to God for this assembly of believers who called me to be their pastor and have faithfully supported my ministry.

I want to thank my friends Eric Anest, Travis Dougherty, and Adam Miller for reading through the chapters and offering many helpful comments. I also want to thank Jim Holmes, whose vision for these studies saw them as two books instead of one. Peter Adam, Iain Campbell, David Jackman, Peter Lewis, Simon Manchester, Josh Moody, and Doug O'Donnell took time out of their busy schedules to read through the manuscript and offer encouraging endorsements. Many thanks to you, my dear brothers.

As always, none of my studying, preaching, teaching, or writing could take place without the help of my dear wife,

Theresa. She patiently puts up with me as I live with my nose in a book.

Most of all, I thank my Lord Jesus Christ, who put me on the pilgrim path and counted me faithful, putting me into the ministry.

Rhett Dodson

August 2012

Your blessed life now

Blessed is everyone who fears the Lord,
who walks in his ways!
You shall eat the fruit of the labor of your hands;
you shall be blessed, and it shall be well with you.
Your wife will be like a fruitful vine
within your house;
your children will be like olive shoots
around your table.
Behold, thus shall the man be blessed
who fears the Lord.
The Lord bless you from Zion!
May you see the prosperity of Jerusalem
all the days of your life!
May you see your children's children!
Peace be upon Israel!

Psalm 128

Over the past couple of years, I've noticed that a lot of people say "Have a blessed day!" I'm not surprised when I hear it said to me at church. In that context, I assume the person is expressing that he or she wants me to have a day filled with the goodness and happiness of God. But I am surprised to hear this expression at the grocery store or the gas station. When I hear it in a nonreligious setting, I ask myself, "Is this person a believer? Does he or she understand what it means to be blessed? Or has this person simply heard this saying, thought it sounded nice, and developed a habit of saying it?" Could an unsaved person really wish you to have a blessed day? If the person who says this is a believer, how does he or she know that I am one too, and could he, she, or I ever say this to an unbeliever?

Hopefully, you would never say, "Have a nasty, unhappy, miserable day!" But what does it mean to have a "blessed day"? And not just a day: what does it mean to have a blessed life? The Lord gave us Psalm 128 to answer that question. The words "blessed" or "bless" occur a total of four times in this text. The psalm is quite obviously about receiving the benefits that God bestows on his people.

What kind of person does God bless? We're told twice, first in verse 1 and then again in verse 4, that the Lord bestows his blessing on those who fear him. Understanding the fear of God is the key to unlocking this psalm, and it's the key to understanding the joy of the Christian life.

Everyone who fears the Lord is blessed. That's Psalm 128 in a nutshell. We need, however, to capture in our minds just what that means. God has dedicated himself to making you happy, but he knows that the only way you can be truly happy is in him. So he has provided a way for you to enjoy him, and though it sounds contradictory, that way is to fear him.

Psalm 128 has a very clear-cut structure of two parts (verses 1–3 and verses 4–6). Each section begins with a general statement about how blessed the person is who fears the Lord.

Then, following that declaration, the application becomes very specific.

The Description of Your Blessed Life

"Blessed is everyone who fears the Lord" (v. 1). "Blessed" is a word we toss around quite a bit in Christian circles, but do we realize that we're talking about being happy? That's what this word means. Oh, the benefits, oh, the happiness, oh, the joy that comes to one who fears the Lord! The word "blessed" actually opens the book of Psalms: "Blessed is the man who walks not in the counsel of the wicked" (Ps. 1:1). At the very beginning of this great hymnbook of Israel, the psalmist strikes the note of happiness for a song of joy.

This is a song we should all be ready to sing because everyone wants to be happy. Even those folk who seem to derive their happiness from being miserable are miserable because they think it will somehow make them happy. But if you want real happiness, it must be fueled by fear.

That statement may sound ridiculous at first, but that's exactly what God is teaching us in this passage. Happy is everyone who fears the Lord. If we want to appreciate how fear can fuel happiness, we have to understand what kind of fear we're talking about. Fearing God doesn't mean being scared in the way you might react to a horror movie, but it includes real fear. Jesus himself told us to be afraid of God because he has the power to cast both our bodies and our souls into hell (Matt. 10:28). Hebrews reminds us that "It is a fearful thing to fall into the hands of the living God" (10:31).

But immediately after telling us to be afraid of what can happen to us, the Lord Jesus reminds us that God is all-knowing and all-caring and we should trust him. If he cares for sparrows and has numbered the hairs on our heads, Jesus says we should "Fear not" (Matt. 10:31). How can Jesus in the same breath say "Be afraid" and "Fear not"? For this reason—Jesus is the one saying it! We should react with terror in the face of God's holiness, his wrath, and our sin. We justly deserve to go to hell. But because of Christ, because he has borne our hell for us on the cross, we can trust God and not be afraid. We learn our first and best lessons in the fear of God at the foot of the cross.[1]

The Old Testament also employs the expression "the fear of the LORD" to describe true, heart religion. This entails reverence, worship, an awe of God as the One who is majestic in splendor and holiness, and a dread of any sin that would displease him. For this reason, Proverbs calls the fear of the Lord the beginning of wisdom (see 1:7, 29; 9:10; 15:33).

The second half of verse 1 defines the fear of God in a very practical way: it means to walk "in his ways." "Blessed is the man who fears the LORD, who greatly delights in his commandments!" (Ps. 112:1). "Blessed are those whose way is blameless, who walk in the law of the LORD!" (Ps. 119:1). The God-fearing man or woman has a dread of sin and a desire for holiness (see also Prov. 3:7; 8:13; 16:6; 23:17).

At its heart, the fear of the Lord is the believer's reaction to God and the obligations of his covenant. To fear God means to trust him, to respond appropriately to his holy majesty and his holy law. Fearing God is the common Old Testament expression that is the equivalent of the New Testament's call to trust in Christ. Do you have this kind of fear? Can you say that you trust in and revere the Lord? Does walking in his commandments characterize your life?

How do you develop the fear of the Lord? It has to begin with the new birth. Unless the Holy Spirit gives you a new heart to know and love God, you will never fear him in the biblical sense of that expression. But if you are a believer, the fear of the Lord is something you can learn and nurture. In Deuteronomy 4:10, Moses recounts how God spoke to him and said, "Gather the people to me, that I may let them hear my words, so that they may learn to fear me all the days that they live on the earth, and that they may teach their children so." David wrote, "Oh, fear the LORD, you his saints, for those who fear him have no lack ... Come, O children, listen to me; I will teach you the fear of the LORD" (Ps. 34:9, 11). How is he going to teach this fear? Through Scripture.

Are you daily getting into God's Word, not just to fulfill your obligations, not just to answer questions for a Bible study, but to know the Lord? The more you discover through the gospel what God is for you in Christ, the more you will fear him and the happier you will be, because you will look for your joy in him.

This kind of fear fuels happiness because it drives you away from sin. Your goal should be to grow in your fear of the

Lord so that when temptation comes knocking at your door you say, “How could I ever commit this sin when I walk with such a great God?” (see Gen. 39:9). This is to say to the Lord, “I treasure you above all things!” and to say to sin, “You are worthless!”

From this kind of life comes great fruitfulness. You will be able to work and enjoy the results of your labor (v. 2). You will have a wife who bears children who are strong, healthy, and flourishing. They “will be like olive shoots around your table” (v. 3). Here is work and home life filled to the brim with happiness as a result of the blessing of God (compare with Ps. 127).

“Have faith in God, and your life will be great! You will have your best life now!” Is that what we should take away from this passage? Is the author of this psalm a health-and-wealth evangelist? Does the Bible teach a prosperity gospel?

What God promises here reflects the blessings guaranteed in Deuteronomy 8 and 28 (a full pantry and a full house). But is this true for everyone? Is Psalm 128 an absolute guarantee, and are we not all healthy and wealthy because we just don’t have enough faith? Could the broad-grinning, slick-talking TV preachers be right after all?

Well, what about Jesus? He had no home (Luke 9:58) and depended on support from others during his public ministry (Matt. 27:55). We have no record that Paul was ever married or had children. The missionary David Brainerd died at age twenty-nine before he could marry the daughter of Jonathan Edwards.

Robert Murray M'Cheyne was a Scottish pastor known as the Saintly M'Cheyne. He never married and also died when he was twenty-nine. Did all these people not fear God?

How are you going to read this passage when you've lost your job? When you can't have children? When you're following God with all your heart, and your life is falling apart? Is this a watertight guarantee that everything will go great if you just fear the Lord?

To answer these questions, we have to put this psalm in its two contexts. First, this is a wisdom psalm. The wisdom literature of the Bible teaches us about the skills of godly living. For example, "The fear of the LORD is the beginning of wisdom" (Prov. 1:7; 9:10). The wise man or woman begins all his or her thinking and acting with reference to God. Wisdom literature, by its nature, speaks in general terms about life. It is *descriptive* not *predictive*. We should not read this passage and think that believers under the Old Covenant had it much easier than we do. Remember Job: he feared God, turned from evil, and suffered greatly. So to understand this psalm we need to put it in its literary context.

We also need to put it in its redemptive–historical context. God promised these blessings of hearth and home to Israel in the promised land if they obeyed him. But like all God's dealings with his covenant nation, these promises of material and familial blessing were preparatory. They were types and shadows. God was paving the way to Christ. Because he was doing this with the Old Testament, we should expect what we read in it to point us in the direction of the New Testament. So jobs and food and wives and children, as the blessings of the covenant, forecast greater blessings to come. They point beyond themselves. If we have hope only in jobs and spouses and children, we are of all people most miserable. But we have a hope that is greater than these things. These material blessings promised to the faithful Israelite serve as signposts. As wonderful as these are, the ultimate banquet and the ultimate family gathering is the marriage supper of the Lamb (Rev. 19:7–9).

When the Lord Jesus returns, he will assemble at this great feast all those who fear the Lord. What Psalm 128 promises to a God-fearing believer under the old system pales into insignificance compared with what God has prepared for us in his presence. The way to have your blessed life now is to tap into the joys of your blessed life to come. The text describes this blessed life in terms of material blessing—pointing us to heaven, to glory. But this blessed life comes from Zion—pointing us to God.

The Source of Your Blessed Life

The second half of the psalm also begins with a general statement: "Behold, thus shall the man be blessed who fears the LORD" (v. 4). These words are very similar, but not identical, to those in verse 1. However, though translated the same way in English, a new Hebrew word for "blessed" comes into play in verse 4, and with the change in terminology comes a slight shift in emphasis. Now it is not just "Oh, how happy is the person who fears the Lord!" though that is still true, but "Behold—pay attention to this! God bestows great benefits on those who find in him their all in all!"

God's blessings came from Zion, the location of the temple (v. 5). The priests pronounced this benediction from the temple on all the pilgrims who came to Jerusalem for the feasts (see Ps. 134). But Zion was also the place that connected the sanctuary and the covenant. This is clearly evident in Solomon's prayer of dedication for the temple (1 Kings 8). If Israel failed to fear the Lord and strayed from fulfilling her covenantal obligations, if she suffered famine or deportation to a foreign land for her iniquity, what was she to do? Turn toward the temple on Mount Zion and pray.

The temple was so important to Israel, not because of its beauty or its central location, but because it was the place where God dwelt with man. That temple no longer stands in Jerusalem, but God still dwells with man. He came in the person of his Son, Immanuel, God with us (Isa. 7:14). The New Testament describes our bodies as the temple of the Holy Spirit (1 Cor. 6:19) and the church as a temple made of living stones (1 Peter 2:5), but the temple of temples is Jesus himself (see John 1:14; compare Rev. 21:22). Every blessing God bestows comes through him.

Paul spells out these blessings in Ephesians 1. We're chosen in Christ (v. 4), predestined for adoption as sons in Christ (v. 5), and redeemed in Christ (v. 7). In Christ, we have obtained an inheritance (v. 11). He is the sum and substance of all that God has for us. Everything that can fill you with joy comes from him.

How do we enjoy these blessings? Is there a way we can tap into them? The answer is "Yes, through prayer." The expressions in verses 5 and 6—"The LORD bless you ... May you see ... May you see"—are all words of benediction. It's very possible that a priest spoke these words at the temple. May you see the blessings of the covenant on a corporate level (the prosperity of Jerusalem, v. 5) and on a personal level (v. 6—"may you live long enough to see your children's children"). Here is a blessing for the nation and the home. But this benediction is set in the context of prayer.

Any Israelite could offer this prayer for blessing, but it was most likely the prayer of a priest. And it still is. This is what Christ prays for us. He prays that we might experience all the benefits that come when the promises of the covenant intersect with a heart that worships and honors him. Read Jesus's High Priestly prayer in John 17 and you'll see that that is exactly what he asks the Father to give to us. He's praying for our joy. He's asking the Father to unite us and glorify us in him, just as he is one with and glorified with the Father (vv. 13, 22).

Prayer is the key to understanding, appreciating, and experiencing this now. That's why Paul, after he lists all those benefits in Ephesians 1, begins to pray, "May God open your eyes, the eyes of your heart, so that you can see and feel and understand and rejoice in Christ" (see vv. 17–18). Prayer is the way for us to participate. As Christ intercedes for us, we go to him in prayer and tell him that we want to know and enjoy all that he is for us.

Your spiritual life will shrivel up without prayer. Do you have any fruit in your refrigerator? Perhaps you have an apple or orange tucked back in the corner that you intend to enjoy one day. You know it will be good for you. But when you open the fridge, sitting right there, staring you in the face, is leftover lasagna. Your favorite! Perhaps it's a piece of pie or cake. Your mother always taught you that it's a sin to waste food, and you're in favor of following mom's method of sanctification! So the fruit remains, surrounded by the aura of doctor's orders and good intentions. Then one day, back behind a jug of milk, you notice a gray, hairy, shriveled-up blob that used to be fruit, and you realize you've wasted your opportunity.

Is your prayer life vibrant or shriveled? Like that piece of fruit, prayer sort of sits around in your mind surrounded by Scripture commands and good intentions. But so many other things offer more immediate happiness. They keep grabbing your attention, feeding your appetite for pleasure but never giving you any lasting satisfaction or spiritual nourishment. What is it that's keeping you from prayer? What will prevent you from spending time with the Lord this afternoon, this evening, or tomorrow?

When it comes to fearing God, to developing that life of reverent worship and enjoying the blessed life, two things are essential: *Scripture* and *prayer*. We develop this fear through the diligent use of the ordinary means of grace. And both these means are important.

If you bought a new battery for your car, which cable would you attach? Just the black one? If so, you're going to be sitting still for a long time. Would you clamp on just the red one? The car still won't run. But if you connect both, the energy of the battery will be harnessed to the potential of the engine and things will happen. You'll get moving!

The same is true in your walk with God. Will you hook up only the cable of Scripture? That's great. You need it. But what about prayer? Or will you hook up only the cable of prayer? What, then, will guide your prayers? If you fasten your heart onto both, you will link your soul to the power of God, his means of channeling grace and power into your life, and things will happen. You'll get moving spiritually! You will grow in the fear of the Lord. And you will experience *your blessed life now!*

Reflect on These Points

1. *Many of the psalms pronounce blessings upon God's people or recount the benefits of the believing life. The most famous blessings come from the lips of Jesus himself in the Beatitudes (Matt. 5:1–12). These blessings describe the life of God's kingdom people.*
2. *What are the elements of a biblical definition of the fear of God? Do you fear God?*
3. *Do you keep a prayer journal or a list of prayer requests? What are some practical ways that you can develop your prayer life to tap into gospel joy?*
4. *How do Scripture and prayer work together for spiritual growth?*

God's victory over evil

"Greatly have they afflicted me from my youth"—
let Israel now say—
"Greatly have they afflicted me from my youth,
yet they have not prevailed against me.
The plowers plowed upon my back;
they made long their furrows."
The LORD is righteous;
he has cut the cords of the wicked.
May all who hate Zion
be put to shame and turned backward!
Let them be like the grass on the housetops,
which withers before it grows up,
with which the reaper does not fill his hand
nor the binder of sheaves his arms,
nor do those who pass by say,
"The blessing of the LORD be upon you!
We bless you in the name of the LORD!"

Psalm 129

When Israel was brought out of Egypt by such a mighty display of God's power, she expected a relatively conflict-free journey to the promised land. This becomes evident in her attitude to obstacles in the wilderness. God's decisive victory over Pharaoh's army, when the Lord divided the Red Sea for Israel to pass safely through but made that same sea a watery grave for her enemies, would have only reinforced this conviction.

But life is never as easy as we think it's going to be. Some moments, things go well. Living seems as effortless as Moses's raising his staff and Egypt's elite forces sinking to the bottom of the sea. But those moments are short-lived. Whatever their thoughts of smooth sailing, the Israelites were not long on the journey before they encountered hunger (Exod. 16:1–3), thirst (17:1–7), and other enemies, like the Amalekites (17:8–16).

Moses doesn't tell us why Amalek attacked Israel, only that she did. We do know that the evil of Amalek brought destruction and heartache. At times, Amalek prevailed in battle (Exod. 17:11). And if she prevailed, then that night, mothers and widows wept in the Israelite camp. While we don't know what provoked the attack, we do know that Israel's enemies were a projection of evil. Amalek was a symptom of the deeper issue of hostility that lies between the kingdom of God and the kingdom of darkness.

Amalek did not win the battle. Moses stood with his hands raised, holding the staff of God. As long as he raised his hands, in a symbolic act of dependence upon the Lord, a symbolic act of prayer, Israel prevailed. Eventually, he sat with his arms supported by Aaron and Hur. Finally, with the staff of God raised on high until sunset, Joshua defeated the Amalekites.

Israel's conflict with Amalek provides us with a model made of three pieces: conflict, prayer, and victory. That same pattern occurs in Psalm 129. Israel has suffered affliction, but she prays with the hope that God will prevail over her enemies.

In this psalm, Israel confesses, "I have been afflicted, but I can have comfort and hope." This prayer expresses the comfort and hope of all God's people. In spite of all that sin and wickedness can do, the Lord will triumph over evil.

Divine Power

The psalm unfolds for us the ways in which God gains victory over evil. First, he breaks the power of sin. The passage begins with a lament, but the words gloriously morph into a declaration of joy, a celebration of God's amazing grace.

We can see the amazing grandeur of God's grace when we set it side by side, as the psalmist does, with Israel's great affliction. He uses the same phrase twice to describe the suffering as *intense*. "Greatly have they afflicted me" (vv. 1–2).

This trouble was also *chronic*. It had been a feature of Israel's history since her youth (v. 2). Since her earliest days out of Egypt, beginning with the Amalekites, Israel faced multiple occasions of conflict and suffering. The Bible gives us a number of examples. All you have to do is read the book of Judges to see the oppression of Moab and the Canaanites, to name only two. Saul and David kept up wars with the Philistines. The Assyrians, who took the northern tribes captive in 722 BC, were so cruel that they mutilated the bodies of their prisoners.

The most graphic imagery of what Israel had to endure comes in verse 3, where we see how *oppressive* this suffering was. "The plowers plowed upon my back; they made long their furrows." The wicked afflicters of Israel were like men going to the field to plow. The ground they broke up, however, was Israel's back. The blade of the plow bit the earth and dug deeply into the soil. The furrows were long. This was severe and extreme suffering.

All this anguish, whether unprovoked, as with Amalek, or justly deserved, as with Assyria or Babylon, plagued Israel throughout her history as a constant reminder of sin and evil. Sin, evil, and suffering are real. Israel's entire story was a witness to this truth.

Divine Intervention

But where affliction, sin, and suffering abounded, grace abounded more (see Rom. 5:20). The first verses of this psalm not only describe Israel's agony, they also describe the Lord's intervention.

Yes, Israel's enemies had tormented her, yet they had not prevailed against her (v. 2). "Yet" is the pivotal word in verse 2. Amalek did her worst. So too did the Philistines, the Assyrians, and the Babylonians. *Yet!* That little word contains big theology. The fact that Israel's afflicters had not prevailed against her testified to the divine purpose. God ruled over all evil as he worked out his plan for his people. For this reason, God could say to the Babylonian exiles, "For I know the plans I have for you, declares the LORD, plans for welfare and not for evil, to give you a future and a hope" (Jer. 29:11).

Yet! History pivots on that little word: the history of Israel, the history of the church, even our own personal history. Had her enemies obliterated Israel, from where would Messiah have come? What would he have come to fulfill?

These first four verses are not just a testimony to the Lord's purpose for Israel, they are also a testimony to the liberating power of God. The righteous Lord has come with decisive action and he "has cut the cords of the wicked" (v. 4). These cords may be the ropes or traces used on a plow (that would make sense in light of v. 3), or they may simply be a way to talk about any type of bondage Israel's enemies used against her. In either case, God had cut the cords and given his people freedom. This could describe Israel's release from Babylonian captivity or any time that the Lord intervened to overthrow evil. To cut the cords of the wicked signifies taking all power from their hands to continue inflicting their cruelty.

This passage presents us with an Old Testament description of the New Testament work of Christ. The death of Jesus breaks the power of sin. Paul wrote in Romans 6:6, "We know that our old self was crucified with him in order that the body of sin might be brought to nothing, so that we would no longer be enslaved to sin." The cross of Christ breaks the reigning power of sin in the life of every believer. How do we know this is true? Paul goes on to say in verse 10, "For the death he died he died to sin, once for all, but the life he lives he lives to God." By taking sin upon himself, Jesus defeated it by his death. The resurrection proves it! The death and resurrection of Christ is the great cord-severing "yet" of redemptive history. Do you believe this truth? Do you realize how much you need it?

You need it when you're tempted. Believing that the person and work of Christ have severed sin's power over you helps you to defeat temptation. "So you also must consider yourselves dead to sin and alive to God in Christ Jesus" (Rom. 6:11). When you're tempted, you have to believe that the gospel is true for you and that you don't have to fall into the sin that entices you. The cross of Christ offers you the power to overcome.

You need it when you suffer. Verse 2 is remarkably similar to something Paul says in 2 Corinthians 4:8–10: "We are afflicted in every way, but not crushed; perplexed, but not driven to despair; persecuted, but not forsaken; struck down, but not destroyed; always carrying in the body the death of Jesus, so that the life of Jesus may also be manifested in our bodies." Paul realizes that suffering is not senseless. Affliction and suffering, carrying about in our bodies the death of Jesus, have the divinely ordained purpose of showing to others the power of the resurrected life of Christ. Every time you suffer persecution, indignity, and pain, it is an opportunity to show to everyone that Christ has been raised from the dead, because it is the opportunity to seek the grace of God in Christ to restrain your pain and trouble and bring you through it with victory. God allows affliction in your life because he wants to show the world the power of the resurrection at work in you.

When you realize that, it will give you an entirely different approach to and outlook on every difficulty you face. Your trials are no longer something to be endured with your teeth gritted and your heart heavy. They are opportunities to say to the whole world, "Jesus lives!"

This great gospel shows us the way to deal with the problem of evil. It teaches us to acknowledge evil as a reality. Sin and wickedness are not social constructs but objective offenses against the holiness of God. Evil does not exist only in our imaginations. The Holocaust, abortion, genocide, terrorism—these are real.

Our problem is that we can define evil, we can illustrate it, we can experience it, and even commit it, but we cannot explain it. It's a mystery. We don't know its origin. We don't know why God allows it, but we do know the solution—the cross. The apostle John put it this way: "The reason the Son of God appeared was to destroy the works of the devil" (1 John 3:8).

Hugh Latimer, a leader of the English Reformation, said that there is "no busier ploughman in all the world than the devil: whoever makes short furrows, he does not."[1] Latimer knew what he was talking about. He served as a chaplain to Edward VI. But when Edward's sister Mary I came to the throne, Latimer fell from favor. Mary's prosecutors examined him regarding his Protestant beliefs and they burned him, along with Nicholas Ridley, at the stake outside Balliol College in Oxford. Yet Latimer knew that his death did not mean the defeat of Christianity. He might die, but the devil would not prevail. As he was strapped to the stake along with Ridley, he said, "Be of good comfort, Master Ridley, and play the man; we shall this day light such a candle, by God's grace, in England, as I trust shall never be put out."[2]

Latimer understood that you can't look at evil from a purely circumstantial perspective. It may appear to get the upper hand for a while. Christianity may seem weak and ineffective. But Christ's death has dealt such a blow to the forces of hell that the church will make steady progress and achieve ultimate triumph at his return. Latimer and Ridley died as martyrs for the faith, but God brought victory to the gospel cause in England.

You may think that the church seems lame, out of touch with the real world, insignificant, and unimportant. You must remember, however, that you are only seeing a snapshot, not the panorama of what God has been doing since he redeemed our first parents. The church may look weak, but looks can be deceiving. Our Lord has defeated and will defeat all evil. And if you take sides against him, you are lining up with the forces that will be damned forever.

Divine Judgment

God breaks the power of evil. That's the first thing this psalm teaches us. But it also teaches us something equally significant: the Lord judges the perpetrators of evil (vv. 5–8).

In the second half of the psalm, we find a description of this judgment, but it occurs in the context of prayer. How do we balance the truth of God's judgment and our prayer for it?

The Lord will judge those "who hate Zion" (v. 5). Hatred is more than rejection. It is a willful, spiteful, loathing of God.

It is intellectual and emotional. Those who hate Zion despise everything that God is for, and they despise God himself.

All who feel this way about the Lord will suffer utter defeat. Verse 5 describes an army that, like a scared dog, has tucked its tail and run! They will "be put to shame and turned backward!"

In 2 Kings 19–20, Sennacherib, king of Assyria, laid siege to Jerusalem with great boasts of victory, only to have the angel of the Lord slay 185,000 of his soldiers during the night. How did he react? "Then Sennacherib king of Assyria departed and went home and lived at Nineveh" (20:36). He was put to shame and turned backward. This is what the Lord is going to do to all his enemies!

Another description of this judgment occurs in verses 6–8 of our psalm. "Let them be like the grass on the housetops" (v. 6). Grass on the roof is probably not an image you're used to thinking about, unless, of course, you forgot to clean your gutters! But what happens when you do forget to do that? Enough dirt gets blown into them that, if some seed also lands there, it sprouts and starts to grow. Now, imagine you live where rooftops are flat and made of mud or clay. A few stray seeds lodge in the cracks and begin to grow. But the roof is hard, not well-plowed ground. So even though the grass starts to grow, it won't last long.

There will be nothing to reap (v. 7), and there will be no celebration (v. 8). No one will pass the field workers and wish them a blessed harvest. The grass withers quickly, with nothing left to gather. Verses 6 through 8 illustrate a swift and complete destruction.

The Lord will bring this kind of judgment on all those who are outside of Christ, all those who hate and oppose him. Paul warned the Corinthians, "If anyone has no love for the Lord, let him be accursed" (1 Cor. 16:22). Do you understand the significance of this? Do you feel the weight of it? If you do not cherish and desire Christ, if you do not have affections that turn toward the Lord Jesus and treasure him above all things, this is the kind of destruction that is coming upon you. If you do not love Christ, cry to him for his saving grace. Ask him to give you a heart that trusts him and truly loves him.

Praying for God's Judgment

Swift and complete destruction: that's what the psalm describes. And this is the very thing the psalmist prays for. Two words are key here: "may" (v. 5) and "let" (v. 6). These words are important because they tell us that all that the psalmist has described about God's judgment is exactly what he prays will happen.

But how can he pray this? How can Israel pray this? Because it is not a personal vendetta. This prayer focuses on Zion because the psalmist's desire is to see the vindication of God's cause. He's praying for the Lord to exercise his justice against evil. He's praying by faith because "the LORD is righteous" (v. 4).

This is not just a prayer for Israel. Christ prays this psalm as well. He is God's Agent of judgment who metes out his justice.

Jesus is the righteous Lord who was afflicted from his youth. He will see the defeat of all his and our enemies.

But this raises the question, "Should you or I ever pray this?" Can we obey the command of Jesus to love our enemies (Matt. 5:43–48; Luke 6:27–37) and still ask the Lord to bring about swift and total destruction on evil? The answer is "Yes," but these prayers must never become self-centered and sinful.

Like the psalmist, we must never pray for personal revenge. Our focus must be the triumph of God's name. You must pray this out of love for God, not out of love for self.

The redemptive–historical context is also important. Psalm 129 pits the kingdom of God against the kingdom of Satan. We are praying ultimately for the destruction of Satan and his minions. Jesus taught us to pray, "Your kingdom come" (Matt. 6:10). To pray this necessarily implies praying for the destruction of Satan's kingdom.

Praying this way is similar to praying for someone with a disease. Francis and Edith Schaeffer were returning from furlough in America to their ministry in Switzerland when they noticed symptoms of polio in their youngest child. They knew what this disease could do. So they prayed for that disease to be totally destroyed, to be eradicated quickly and completely from his little body so that he could be spared.[3]

That's how we should pray against evil. We cannot love our enemies unless we utterly detest, hate, and wish for the destruction of the very thing that will destroy them. We do not pray for God's victory over evil because we take delight in the destruction of our opponents (see Ezek. 18:23). We desire first and foremost their salvation.

When Jesus died on the cross, it appeared that evil had gotten the upper hand, that Satan had finally triumphed, and that God had been defeated. The dark hours that shrouded Golgotha seemed to envelop the world in darkness forever. But what seemed to be Satan's triumph proved to be God's decisive victory. When Jesus cried out, "It is finished" (John 19:30), that rugged Roman cross was transformed into the victory chariot that led the parade of the King of kings (Eph. 4:8; Col. 2:15)!

We know that's true because three days later, God raised Jesus from the dead! The resurrection was the ultimate announcement of victory over evil. One day, God will make the final announcement. An archangel will shout. A trumpet will sound. The Lord Jesus himself will come (1 Thes. 4:16–17). Then all that we have hoped in and all that we have prayed for will come to pass. Evil will have tried to do its worst to us, but on that day our song will be, "Thanks be to God who gives us the victory through our Lord Jesus Christ" (1 Cor. 15:57).

Is that your comfort and hope?

Reflect on These Points

1. *God not only displayed his power against Amalek; his decisive victory at Jericho proved beyond all doubt to Israel and the Canaanites that God fought for his people. God still fights for and defends his chosen ones.*
2. *What trial are you currently experiencing in your life? How does Christ's resurrection shed new light on it?*
3. *It is a good and godly act to pray against evil. Do not let the prevailing sentiments of the world convince you otherwise.*
4. *The closing words of the psalm are similar to the greeting found in Ruth 2:4. The joyful harvest and the firstfruits of the harvest remind believers of Jesus, the firstfruits of the resurrection (1 Cor. 15:20).*

Out of the depths

Out of the depths I cry to you, O LORD!
O Lord, hear my voice!
Let your ears be attentive
to the voice of my pleas for mercy!
If you, O LORD, should mark iniquities,
O Lord, who could stand?
But with you there is forgiveness,
that you may be feared.
I wait for the LORD, my soul waits,
and in his word I hope;
my soul waits for the Lord
more than watchmen for the morning,
more than watchmen for the morning.
O Israel, hope in the LORD!
For with the LORD there is steadfast love,
and with him is plentiful redemption.
And he will redeem Israel
from all his iniquities.

Psalm 130

The story of John Wesley's conversion holds a prominent place in the chronicles of church history. Wesley recounts that on a May evening in 1738 he attended a meeting at Aldersgate, where he heard someone read Martin Luther's preface to the book of Romans. During that reading, Wesley found his heart "strangely warmed." That evening, he trusted in Christ alone for his salvation.

What is less well known is that earlier that same day, Wesley attended St. Paul's Cathedral, where he heard the choir sing Psalm 130.[1] On that spring day, the truth of Psalm 130 and the clear exposition of the gospel in Romans joined forces to captivate the soul of Methodism's founder. These two passages worked together in Wesley's heart because, in essence, Psalm 130 teaches in embryonic form the message of Romans.

Someone once asked Martin Luther, "Which are the best psalms?" Luther replied, "The psalms of Paul!" The psalms of Paul? Which are they? He answered that they were Psalms 32, 51, 130, and 143, four of the seven penitential psalms.[2] These psalms express the heart and desires of a person under conviction of sin. They also drive the penitent to God for forgiveness. In fact, Paul uses Psalm 32 extensively in Romans 4 as the scriptural basis for teaching the doctrine of justification by faith alone.

Psalm 130 not only played an important role in Wesley's life and serves as a paradigm of Luther's life, as it recounts his climb from the depths of woe and misery to the joy of salvation; it also provides a vision statement for the church, as it magnifies the grace of God in salvation in order to bring glory to the name of Christ. The words of verse 4 capture the central theme of the psalm: "But with you there is forgiveness, that you may be feared." In other words, God gives the grace of forgiveness in order to receive the glory of worship. That statement summarizes the message of this psalm, and outlines it as well.

The Grace of Forgiveness

The topic of forgiveness dominates the first four verses. We see the term "forgiveness" itself in verse 4, and the related themes of "pleas for mercy" in verse 2 and "marking iniquities" in verse 3. But the psalmist begins with cries. Can you hear the need and anguish in his voice? "I cry to you, O LORD! O Lord, hear my voice! Let your ears be attentive to the voice of my pleas for mercy!" (v. 2). Here stands a soul in life-and-death intercession with God. This is not playacting, nor is it religion with a flair for the dramatic. This is earnest and urgent prayer.

Our psalmist cries out from the "depths." In the Old Testament, this expression usually describes the deep waters of the sea, but here the use is metaphorical. He's going through deep waters. He's in distress, and the context indicates that these circumstances result from his sin. We can see this from the end of verse 2, where his continual cries from the depths are pleas for mercy and have to do with his iniquities (see also v. 3). These cries of distress come from an inescapable place. The depths are the very place where you need God to meet you with his grace.

These pleas not only express a broken heart, they also express a resolute faith. To whom does the psalmist cry? He calls out to Jehovah. He calls him "My Master"—that's another translation of the word given as "Lord" at the beginning of verse 2. He begs that God will hear.

The Forgiveness of God

What if God kept a record of our sins? Could any of us defend ourselves before him?

As we move into the second section of the psalm, we find ourselves transitioning from cries of desperation to a rhetorical question: "If you, O LORD, should mark iniquities, O Lord, who could stand?" (v. 3). We're all guilty of iniquity. We've all gone our crooked, twisted ways that have ignored and flouted God's law. We've deviated from the path of righteousness. We've sinned again and again. We too often talk about mistakes and bad decisions. God's Word talks about evil, wickedness, and vice—iniquity. Scripture describes our sin as filthiness in the sight of a pure and spotless God. If God should mark even one of our sins, could any of us stand in his sight?

What lies behind this question? The holiness of God. He is so pure, his divine perfections are so absolute and infinite, that he cannot abide even the hint of a sin in his presence. Nothing spiritually or morally unclean, no sin or iniquity, no trespass or violation of his holy law, can or will go unnoticed.

And God does keep a record of sin. When John saw the sixth seal of the great book of history opened, he saw the coming judgment and wrath of God. People were crying out for the mountains and rocks to hide them from the wrath of the Lamb. "For the great day of their wrath has come, and who can stand?" (Rev. 6:17). Who can stand? That's the psalmist's question. It's the question we should be asking ourselves. *What will it be like for me when I am face-to-face with God?*

These cries reflect much of the early life of Martin Luther. One day, when Luther was returning to school, he was caught in a severe thunderstorm. Frightened, he took shelter under a tree and cried out, “Saint Anne, help me! I will become a monk!” But when he entered the Augustinian monastery, he found himself confronted not with the saints of the church, but with the holy God of heaven. How could he ever stand before a holy God? He tried to be an obedient son of the church. He fasted often. He beat his body. He spent hours confessing his sins to Father Staupitz, his spiritual director. He studied his Bible. He prayed. But nothing he did gave him the peace he sought. Nothing could give him the assurance that he was forgiven until the Lord opened his eyes to the gospel and the truth that the just shall live by faith (Rom. 1:16–17). He discovered that there is forgiveness with the Lord.[3]

God marks iniquities. He knows every sin that we commit, and holds each of us accountable for each sin. But you can have the record expunged. God can wipe the slate clean so that he never holds any of your sins against you. That’s what Luther discovered, and that’s what you need to discover and rediscover again and again.

What does God do with our iniquity? How can he know all our sins and yet not hold them against us? Another way to ask this question is, “How can a holy God ever pardon unholy sinners?” He can’t say, “Let’s just forget about it.” He can’t ignore it. He must maintain his inflexible holiness and yet be full of grace. And in his wisdom, God has chosen to do this by sending his Son (1 Cor. 1:18–25). Jesus Christ came to bear the penalty of the broken law. He came to be punished in our place, to bear our sins on the cross and suffer God's wrath so that the holy Lord could remain holy and yet reach out his hand of love and mercy to us (see Rom. 3:24–26).

Have you experienced this salvation? If not, follow the psalmist's example. Cry out to the Lord for his saving mercy. Christ promises that "Everyone who calls on the name of the Lord will be saved" (Rom. 10:13). Look to Christ as your only hope, and you will find that you have hope for today and for eternity.

You will have hope for the day of judgment. Remember John's vision when he saw the sixth seal opened? After he cried out like the psalmist, "Who can stand?", he saw 144,000 whom God had sealed as his own (Rev. 7:1–8). He then saw a great multitude that no one could number, from every nation (vv. 9–10). Here is the Israel of God, the elect, the church of Jesus Christ. And what are they doing? They're "standing before the throne and before the Lamb, clothed in white robes, with palm branches in their hands, and crying out with a loud voice, 'Salvation belongs to our God who sits on the throne, and to the Lamb!'" They're standing; they're worshiping because they are standing in Christ!

This psalm reflects what that scene in heaven is all about. Great salvation leads to great worship. Verse 4 closes with a purpose statement. With the Lord there is forgiveness so that he may be feared. God saves us so that he will have worshipers who fear him. Yes, salvation gives us a home in heaven, and it gives us a purpose for living now. It puts life in perspective and joy in our hearts. It does all of that and a thousand other things. But all those benefits are secondary. First and foremost, it gets us to God. Why did Jesus come? "For Christ also suffered once for sins, the righteous for the unrighteous, that he might bring us to God" (1 Peter 3:18).

If what you call salvation has not led you to the feet of Jesus to worship and adore him for his marvelous glory, beauty, and grace, what you have is not saving grace. It may be religion. It may use Christian vocabulary. But if it doesn't leave you humble and grateful and glorying in Jesus alone, it is empty religion and will take you to hell.

The Glory of Worship

If you know Christ, if God has redeemed you and made you his child, he has made you a worshiper. The second half of this psalm explains what that involves.

The tone changes in this section. Crying out for mercy and receiving forgiveness lead to waiting in hope and encouraging the people of God to hope in the Lord. This is the life of worship. This is the glory of worship.

Few people enjoy waiting patiently, but true worship requires us to do just that. "I wait for the Lord … my soul waits … my soul waits." The believer who waits for God looks with eager expectation and hope that the Lord will act on his or her behalf. We look for him to do what he has promised. When a person waits on God, he or she hopes "in his word" (v. 5).

The psalmist then draws a comparison between the way he waits on the Lord and the way watchmen wait for the morning. In the ancient world of walled cities, watchmen patrolled the tops of city walls to sound an alarm in the event of an enemy attack. Watchmen eagerly wait for morning light, because during the darkness of the night a city is more vulnerable. It is more difficult to see the enemy approach. When the light of dawn first breaks over the horizon, a sense of relief pours over the watchmen. The night has passed. All is safe. This comparison also conveys a sense of hope. The watchmen are sure that the morning will come. The sun will rise in the morning as surely as it set the previous day.

Waiting on God is not a passive pursuit. This is not waiting-room waiting, where you sit and mindlessly thumb through a magazine. This is watchtower waiting.

Waiting on the Lord is really synonymous with praying. How do we eagerly look for something from God? We ask for it. And we ask again and again and again. Jesus taught us, "Ask, and it will be given to you; seek, and you will find; knock, and it will be opened to you" (Matt. 7:7).

When we pray, we acknowledge that we have no control over the destiny of our lives. We've experienced that when it comes to illness. No illness ever strikes at a convenient time. We have no control over so many of the things that happen to us.

It's imperative, then, that we seek the Lord, through his Word and prayer, to act for us. The Word and prayer keep our souls engaged with God. When we wait on him, he wants to hear his living voice echoed in ours. One of the primary ways, then, to wait on him is to pray the Scriptures. If you're serious about real, faith-filled worship, start praying the psalms. Take what God says and echo it back to him in prayer. If he says that the person is blessed who doesn't walk in the counsel of the ungodly, nor stand in the way of sinners, nor sit in the seat of scoffers (Ps. 1:1), ask him to make you that blessed person who turns from sin and seeks his face. Then move to the next verse and on through the psalm.

I fear that far too much of the evangelical church has lost this vision for Scripture-saturated prayer. We use casual phrases to express felt needs rather than biblical phrases to honor God. Will you be a believer who prays the Bible?

Gospel Worship

True worship always focuses on the person and work of Christ. In the last two verses, the psalmist not only sings of his hope in the Lord, but he also calls out to the whole nation to hope in him as well. "O Israel, hope in the LORD!" (v. 7). Invest all your aspirations in him!

Why do that? For three good reasons. First, with the Lord there is steadfast love (v. 7). "Steadfast love" is one of the most significant theological terms in the Old Testament. It is a heavily relational term. It is God's covenantal love and loyalty to his people. We can hope in the Lord because he will never turn his love away from us. It is an enduring, endearing love that calls for our worship. "I have loved you with an everlasting love; therefore I have continued my faithfulness to you" (Jer. 31:3).

When we come to Christ, we commit ourselves to him. Behind that commitment, however, lies the eternal commitment of God to bind himself to us in love. This is the love that drew us to Christ, and this is the love that will keep us in Christ.

Second, Israel can hope in the Lord because with him there is plentiful redemption (v. 7). In a very real sense, forgiveness and redemption were not things that Israel had to wait for. They could be for them a present reality. The faithful of Israel experienced this redemption as they looked to their coming Messiah. They knew about forgiveness because the sacrificial system pictured it so accurately and graphically. In addition, the prophets clearly promised that one would come whose wounds would be for the healing of the nations (see, for example, Isa. 53). Plentiful redemption is what God offers us in Christ. You have not committed a sin that, if brought to the cross, will remain unforgiven (Matt. 12:31–32).

Third, we have reason to hope because with the Lord there is coming redemption. The believers in Israel had their sins forgiven. By faith, they looked forward to the coming work of Christ. But in another very real sense, Israel had to wait for her redemption. She had to wait for the fulfillment of the promises of God for her Redeemer to come. This explains the shift from the stative declarations in verse 7 to the future verb in verse 8. With him is redemption, and he shall redeem!

Here the finger of the psalmist points down the corridor

of redemptive history to what Israel anticipated. One was to come who would bring in the fullness of God's saving grace, One who would embody redemption. But the words of verse 8 point beyond the first coming to the culmination of redemptive history, when Jesus comes again. Our Lord will return for the final act of salvation when plentiful redemption bursts forth in eternal glorification.

We engage in real worship by faith, because that's the way our souls interact with God. But real worship is also gospel-focused, because when we come to God, we come to him through the Mediator, our Lord Jesus Christ (1 Tim. 2:5).

The psalmist began as a penitent crying out from the depths. Now, through the grace of salvation, he has become a cantor, calling all the people of God to join him in the song of redemption.

In 1530, Martin Luther lived for a while in the fortress at Coburg. During that time, it seems he suffered from migraine headaches. One night, he saw what appeared to be burning torches pass before his eyes four times. This was probably the aura that migraine sufferers experience. Another night, he saw three lights and fainted. His servant did the best he could. He poured almond oil in his ear and rubbed his feet with hot cloths to stimulate the circulation.

When Luther recovered, he asked his servant to read to him a portion from Galatians, and during the reading he fell asleep. When he awoke, Luther was full of joy and said to his servant, “Come, to spite the devil, let us sing the psalm *De profundis*!”[4]

To spite the devil, let us sing this psalm too. Let’s rehearse it in private and sing it in public. Let it fill our lives, our church services, and our witness with joy, because worship flows from salvation. The more we give glory to God, the more we experience the joy of Christ.

Reflect on These Points

1. *The Lord does not despise the cry of a broken heart. "The sacrifices of God are a broken spirit; a broken and contrite heart, O God, you will not despise" (Ps. 51:17). To offer a humble and broken spirit to him is an act of worship.*
2. *God offers no greater assurance than the full and free forgiveness of sins through Christ. Your assurance of salvation does not depend upon the strength of your faith but on the strength of Christ's work.*
3. *Why do you find it difficult to wait on the Lord? What can you learn from this psalm to help you?*
4. *God's steadfast love endures for eternity. That's the theme of Psalm 136. Read through that psalm and think about the manifold ways God has shown his steadfast love.*

Stressed!

O L*ORD*, *my heart is not lifted up;*
my eyes are not raised too high;
I do not occupy myself with things
too great and too marvelous for me.
But I have calmed and quieted my soul,
like a weaned child with its mother;
like a weaned child is my soul within me.
O Israel, hope in the L*ORD*
from this time forth and forevermore.

Psalm 131

"Will I make it through the next set of cutbacks at work?" "Will I ever pass that history exam?" "The pain in my side keeps getting worse. Is my health going to hold out?" "Where were you? It's past your curfew!" "Another bill!"

Sound familiar?

These, and countless other scenarios of daily life, exert a constant influence on us to acquire and achieve more. Now take the pressures of daily life and mix them with the discontent that so often characterizes our hearts, and you have a recipe for massive amounts of stress. We all suffer from it. You and I can no more live in the twenty-first century and avoid stress than we can breathe and avoid oxygen.

Time magazine called stress "The Epidemic of the Eighties."[1] If only stress had ended with the 1980s! Yet the passage of three decades has not alleviated its difficult and even deadly effects. A survey taken as recently as 1996 revealed that 75 percent of people suffer from stress at least one day a week. Stress is the cause of 75 to 90 percent of the visits people make to their primary care physicians.[2] In 2007, Sylvia Carlson wrote, "One could argue that stress-related health problems are on the rise."[3] We all battle stress. It's not just adults who feel it. Young people also suffer, as cultural and peer pressure to wear the right clothes, buy the latest gadgets, and move in the right circles of friends weighs heavily on them.

If we are honest with ourselves, we can trace much of our problem with stress to a lack of contentment. The pressures of life weigh most heavily on us when we are not satisfied with what the Lord allows us to do, to be, or to have. Circumstances might contribute to our stress, but how do we react in our hearts?

The opposite of stress is calmness. It doesn't take a genius to arrive at that conclusion, but it's the rare person who actually achieves contentment. When Puritan Jeremiah Boroughs wrote *The Rare Jewel of Christian Contentment*, he couldn't have chosen a better title. It is *rare* to find people, especially in our culture, who are calm and content inside. But what a precious *jewel*! How valuable it is to have a peaceful heart. Have you learned to mine this priceless gem?

None of us can live without problems and pressures, but we *can* have a life of contentment and peace. How? We can be content in life if we are willing humbly to trust the purposes of

God. That's what David teaches in Psalm 131. He teaches us how to mine the rare jewel of Christian contentment.

To understand contentment, we have to understand its relationship to three other attitudes and how those attitudes reveal our faith, or unbelief, in the purposes of God. Psalm 131 highlights these relationships, and as we study them we will travel straight through its three verses.

Contentment and Pride

First, David emphasizes the relationship between contentment and pride. These two characteristics are always incompatible. David would never have been able to say, as he does in verse 2, that he had calmed and quieted his soul, had he not first dealt with his pride.

Pride comes as naturally to us as breathing. Let's face it—we all like to think very highly of ourselves, and only diligent spiritual discipline, undergirded by the radical, life-changing grace of God in Christ, can ever triumph over the pride in our hearts. David experienced this grace, so he could write in verse 1, "O Lord, my heart is not lifted up; my eyes are not raised too high; I do not occupy myself with things too great and too marvelous for me."

Like every sin, pride begins in the heart. David writes, "O Lord, my heart is not lifted up." Both Isaiah (3:16) and Ezekiel (28:2) condemn those whose hearts are lifted up within them, whether it be the daughters of Zion or the prince of Tyre. No one is exempt from this sin, but no one has the right to commit it.

A heart lifted up is a heart that has exalted itself in its own estimation. Nothing so characterizes our culture as the hubris of the "I." But this attitude is contrary to a biblical lifestyle. Put very plainly, David says, "I don't think of myself more highly than I ought" (see Rom. 12:3). By God's grace he had taken his heart and pushed it down to a place of humble, submissive reverence before the Lord.

If you have an arrogant heart, it won't take long for everyone to know it. Pride has a way of breaking out all over you like an allergic reaction. Try as you might, you can't hide it. If your heart is arrogant, pretty soon you will have a haughty look. David wrote, "My eyes are not raised too high." Today we would say, "I haven't turned up my nose. I don't go around with a disdainful or contemptuous look. I don't look down on others."

You might be able to masquerade and cover up all kinds of sin, but the sin of pride is harder to hide than any other. Sooner or later, your eyes and your face will reveal what lies deep in your heart. We all have a certain transparency when it comes to this sin. Eventually, everyone will be able to see it. I'm sure you've experienced this in a conversation with someone. The person's words revealed his or her arrogance, and, at the same time, you could see pride written all over his or her face. Remember that experience, because when you have a haughty heart, others can see it in you too.

David had to resist another facet of pride that we struggle with as well—presumption. This led him to write, "I do not occupy myself with things too great and too marvelous for me" (v. 1). What did he mean by this statement? Was he uninterested in achievement? Is it wrong for us to set high goals and strive for them? No, David's great accomplishments during his reign as king of Israel prove that this isn't the case. He doesn't say that he never attempted great things. He had high and godly aspirations, and so should we. David's point is that he did not obsess about things beyond the call and will of God for his life. He busied himself with what God had called him to do and, in so doing, found contentment. He wasn't presumptuous in attempting to do what God hadn't called him to do. In other words, he didn't attempt to overstep the bounds that God had set for him. You and I run into trouble when we chafe against the boundaries of God. Each of us has a unique role to play in God's providential plans. We can lower our stress levels dramatically by simply opening our eyes to the wonder of God's plan, place, and purpose for us as individuals, rather than striving to be like everyone else.

When David refers to the things "too marvelous" for him, he means the wondrous works and plans of God, God's secret counsels. He says, "I don't pry into those either." He satisfies his heart with the word that God has revealed. David lets God mind his own business, and he minds his.

Here is the confession of an honest soul. The temptation, however, is to do the very opposite. Arrogance, haughtiness, and presumption are the easiest sins in the world for us to commit, and they soon lead us to stress and discouragement and, ultimately, our downfall, all because we are not God and yet think we should be. We don't have control over our lives or the lives of others; to act as though we do or should is the first step down a dangerous and deadly path.

Pride is where all the trouble began. Think about it for a minute. Pride got us into this mess of sin in the first place. When Satan tempted Eve, he appealed to her pride. "But the serpent said to the woman, 'You will not surely die. For God knows that when you eat of it your eyes will be opened, and you will be like God, knowing good and evil'" (Gen. 3:4–5).

What an appealing proposition! Eve began to think that she should have the same rights as God, that she should be able to say what's right and what's wrong. Nothing puts us into a spiritual tailspin faster than pride. First, we begin to think we're better than we are. Then we begin to look down on others whom we perceive are worse than we are. Finally, we presume that we deserve a certain position or certain possessions. What does all of this lead to? Incredible dissatisfaction and stress! It leads to a chaotic soul, one that says, "God, you're not doing what I want you to do or what I think you should do." Pride leads us into sin, and there is pride in every sin we commit. As long as we think that we should be in charge and life should work out according to *our* plans, we'll never be content.

If pride causes all our problems, humility provides the solution. That, too, might sound overly simplistic, but the source of our salvation, the source of our deliverance from pride and distrust, is the humility of Jesus Christ. When Paul wrote to the Philippians, he urged them to humble themselves based on the saving humility of the Lord Jesus:

> Do nothing from selfish ambition or conceit, but in humility count others more significant than yourselves. Let each of you look not only to his own interests, but also to the interests of others. Have this mind among yourselves, which is yours in Christ Jesus, who, though he was in the form of God, did not count equality with God a thing to be grasped, but emptied himself, by taking the form of a servant, being born in the likeness of men. And being found in human form, he humbled himself by becoming obedient to the point of death, even death on a cross. (Phil. 2:3–8)

The way to have your sins forgiven is to submit humbly to God's way of salvation in Christ. The way to defeat your pride and come to a place of contentment is to have the mind of Christ, a mind that humbles itself before others rather than exalting itself over God and others. The only way to have this mind, this outlook, is to go to the foot of the cross. When your heart begins to recognize what Jesus did to save you, the Holy Spirit uses that truth to defeat pride in you and bring you to a place of submission before the Lord.

Contentment and Calmness

Now we need to examine a second relationship. If contentment and pride are mutually *exclusive*, contentment and calmness are mutually *inclusive*. This truth stands out in the comparison David draws in verse 2: "But I have calmed and quieted my soul, like a weaned child with its mother; like a weaned child is my soul within me."

"But ..." In contrast to someone who is arrogant and haughty, David can honestly say, "I have calmed and quieted my soul" (v. 2). Many of us might look at such a statement and admire David's self-discipline. Yet if we think of his confession only in terms of self-mastery, we have failed to grasp his main point.

To describe just what he means, David compares his calmed and quieted soul to a weaned child sitting on his or her mother's lap. The best way to understand this comparison is to ask, "How does an *unweaned* child act?" The answer is that he or she fusses, frets, and squirms, whimpering and crying because of the need to feed. A *weaned* child, by contrast, is calm, not fussing, not anxious. He or she sits quietly, resting on the mother's lap. This is a description of David's soul—calm and collected.

This analogy reminds me of an incident that happened several years ago when I boarded a plane for a flight from Detroit, Michigan, to my home in Greenville, South Carolina. I found my window seat, settled in to read, and hoped that the flight would not be full so that the two seats next to me would remain unoccupied. Just as I began to read, a lady and her baby boarded and began to walk down the aisle. The baby was screaming. I don't mean that the baby was crying; he was *screaming*, providing stiff competition for the decibels of the jet's engines. "Please, Lord," I began to pray, "please don't let them sit next to me." Guess where they sat!

As the lady approached my row, she was juggling her purse, carry-on luggage, a diaper bag, and the screaming baby. Trying to remember that I was a Christian, I asked her if I could do anything to help. With a haggard look of desperation on her face and a near-exhausted sound in her voice, she asked, "Would you please hold my baby?"

Passing the baby from mommy to an ugly stranger proved to be no cure for the screaming, and I turned to see everyone on the plane staring at me. I wanted to stand up and shout, "This is not *my* baby!" Shouting, however, would have been completely futile at that point. No shouting that I was capable of could ever compete with the screaming. *This is going to be a long flight*, I thought.

The mother arranged her gear as quickly as she could, took her seat, fumbled through the diaper bag, and produced a jar of unnaturally colored mush labeled "Baby Food." She dipped a spoon into the jar and shoved the food into the baby's mouth. Suddenly, the baby went from screaming to a few snorts and sniffles, and he was quiet for the rest of the flight! That contrast between screaming and quietness is what David is talking about in verse 2. Once that mother fed her baby, he was calm and quiet. He was content, because his basic need for food was met. He ate, he settled down, and he slept.

In essence, verse 2 is David's confession: "I am at rest." When we understand what David says, we realize that there are theological links in verse 2 that we dare not miss, links that pull together both ends of the Bible. Here we find theological connections to God's rest, Sabbath rest, and resting in Jesus.

When the Lord rested at the end of the creation week (see Gen. 2:2), was he tired? Did God rest so that he could recuperate his energy? Of course not. What, then, does the text mean when it says that he rested? To answer that question, just look at the context of the creation week. Throughout that week, God made things and then said, "That's good!" (Gen. 1:4, 10, 12, 18, 21, 25). At the end of the sixth day, God looked at all that he had made and said, "That's very good!" (Gen. 1:31). When the Lord rested on the seventh day, his rest was a reflection of his contentment and satisfaction with all that he had made.

This is a key facet of Sabbath rest for believers. We set aside a day to testify that we are content with what God allows us to do and earn the other six days of the week, and therefore we do not have to work nonstop to greedily grasp all that we can get (see Isa. 58:13–14).

Salvation comes when we rest in Jesus. So many people are stressed about so many things and fail to realize that the greatest pressure in their lives is the weight of the sin and guilt that they carry before God. However, a person who has been forgiven and who has faith in the Lord Jesus Christ is satisfied with the work Christ has done for his or her salvation. The author of Hebrews highlights this truth when he explains that the "rest" of the promised land that Israel looked forward to was not the ultimate end that God had in mind (see Heb. 3:7–4:13). Joshua, although a great leader, could never guide the people of God into eternal rest. It took a greater Joshua—Jesus—to accomplish the "rest" of our salvation (Heb. 4:8–10). Are you content with the work of Christ? Are you resting in Jesus to forgive you, redeem you, and take you to heaven—or are you frantically trying to do things to earn God's smile?

If you are content with Christ's work for your salvation, are you discontented with other areas of your life? Why are we so often dissatisfied? We could give many answers to that question. You might be disappointed because you want to be someone great, well known, and respected, and yet you seem to be a nobody. Jeremiah had a servant named Baruch who thought like this. He must have been an aspiring and ambitious young man, because the Lord had to say to him, "And do you seek great things for yourself? Seek them not ..." (Jer. 45:5). God might have you in an out-of-the-way place or in a very difficult, no-thanks kind of job, and you're not very happy about it. Are you saying, "Lord, you don't know what you're doing?"

Another reason we are so often dissatisfied is because of our obsession with material goods. We have far too many things and far too many choices in our consumerist culture.

When you multiply choices, you multiply discontentment. You would think that many things and many choices would make people happy and satisfied, yet it does just the opposite.

Several years ago, I went shopping for a watch. I didn't think that this would be a big deal. My Timex ticked its last tick, and I thought I'd buy something a little nicer than my old $30 watch. That's where all the trouble began. Do you have any idea how many different kinds of watches are for sale in jewelry and department stores? I suddenly found myself overwhelmed with the choices. It was a bit mind-numbing. I finally said to one saleslady, "There should be a gold watch and a silver watch, a black band and a brown band, and nothing more." Choices beyond that were too much for me. To my own shame, I bought and returned three watches. With so many choices, I couldn't be satisfied with any of them. Finally, I bought—and kept—a $30 Timex!

You and I grow discontented when we begin to fall prey to the idolatrous lie that things will make us happy. Television tells us that they will. Billboards tell us the same story. Our friends and family tout the same ideas, and we even lie to ourselves. Yet everyone who tries to find satisfaction in possessions always finds that he or she needs just a little more to be *really* happy.

We manufacture stress because we're full of pride, we think we know best, and we're not content with what God is doing in our lives. What are we saying when we're stressed and dissatisfied? We're saying, "Christ, you're not enough for me." The root of our problem is spiritual. That applies not just to stress and discontentment with your job and your possessions, but also to your marriage, your relationships with your children, and your relationships with your fellow Christians and your church.

Verse 2 leads us to face some serious questions that demand honest answers: is Christ enough for you? Are your heart and mind at rest? Are you satisfied with Christ for the forgiveness of sins? Or are you stressed, trying to do more and be more to earn God's love and favor? If you are a Christian, are you content with God's purposes for your life? Are you happy with what God gives you? None of us should answer these questions too quickly or thoughtlessly, but we *must* answer them.

If Christ is enough for you, you can say, "I have calmed and quieted my soul, like a weaned child with its mother; like a weaned child is my soul within me." That kind of attitude leads to a whole new outlook on life. It leads us to hope, and to desire to share that hope with others.

Contentment and Hope

The third and final set of truths in this psalm deals with contentment and hope. These two characteristics are twins. If you are content with the purposes of God, you have great hope that all will be well. This psalm, like Psalm 130, concludes with a corporate call to faith: "O Israel, hope in the LORD from this time forth and forevermore" (v. 3; see 130:7).

Psalm 130:7 gives the reason to hope in the Lord—with him is "steadfast love" and "plentiful redemption." Psalm 131 emphasizes the duration and continuing validity of trusting in the Lord. David presents us with both a present and a future hope. The solution to life's stresses will never change. Our only hope is to trust in the Lord now and forever. This summons to trust in the Lord comes from a deep and profound encounter with God himself, an encounter that led David to turn from his pride and arrogance and to content himself with the purposes of God in his life.

"Hope" is a key term in the believer's vocabulary. It's the sum and substance of our faith (see Eph. 1:18). Biblical hope is not a maybe-so kind of hope that says, "I hope (maybe) to have a relaxing vacation this summer." Biblical hope is certainty. Hope is the Christian's guarantee from God. It is rooted in Christ (see 1 Tim. 1:1) and will find its fullest realization when he comes again, an event that Paul calls our "blessed hope" (Titus 2:13). When David urges us to hope in the Lord, he is calling us to turn from all the disrupting and discouraging pressures that divert us from our calling to follow Christ and Christ alone. Derek Kidner summarized it best when he wrote, "The last verse rouses us from contemplating David to following his example and that of his greater Son: not through introspection but through being weaned from insubstantial ambitions to the only solid fare that can be ours. 'My food is to do the will of him who sent me, and to accomplish his work' (John 4:34)."[4]

Be Still, My Soul

When you think about the message of this psalm, what is it saying if not this:

> Be still, my soul: the Lord is on thy side.
> Bear patiently the cross of grief or pain.
> Leave to thy God to order and provide;
> In every change, He faithful will remain.
> Be still, my soul: thy best, thy heavenly Friend
> Through thorny ways leads to a joyful end.
> (Katharina A. von Schlegel, 1752)

The film *Chariots of Fire* brought to a new generation the story of the heroic courage and conviction of Eric Liddell. Liddell was a gold medalist in the 1924 Olympics but went on, not to seek wealth and fame from a career in sports, but to become a missionary in China. Captured during World War II, Liddell taught "Be Still, My Soul," his favorite hymn, to his fellow prisoners. He spent his last days as a prisoner of war, eventually dying from a brain tumor.[5]

As a gold medalist, Liddell had the world at his feet, yet he humbled himself to be a servant of Christ. Rather than running free as an Olympic athlete, he found himself imprisoned. But what a free soul: a soul like a weaned child resting in the arms of Jesus.

This psalm holds out to you the opportunity to overcome

stress and anxiety. Really! The arms of Christ have the strength to hold you. You can rest there. Cast yourself into those arms, and surrender yourself completely to be, to do, and to have what he wants for your life. Rest in his arms, satisfied with Jesus.

Reflect on These Points

1. *What causes you stress? Why do you think it puts such an emotional strain on you?*
2. *What are some of the telltale signs of pride? Do you detect any of them in your life?*
3. *God has given you a day of rest, the Lord's Day, the Christian Sabbath, to help relieve you of stress. Observing the Lord's Day is one of the main ways to keep your spiritual and emotional equilibrium.*
4. *David could confess to God a calm and quiet spirit. Can you?*

Seeking God's presence

Remember, O LORD, in David's favor,
all the hardships he endured,
how he swore to the LORD
and vowed to the Mighty One of Jacob,
"I will not enter my house
or get into my bed,
I will not give sleep to my eyes
or slumber to my eyelids,
until I find a place for the LORD,
a dwelling place for the Mighty One of Jacob."
Behold, we heard of it in Ephrathah;
we found it in the fields of Jaar.
"Let us go to his dwelling place;
let us worship at his footstool!"
Arise, O LORD, and go to your resting place,
you and the ark of your might.
Let your priests be clothed with righteousness,
and let your saints shout for joy.
For the sake of your servant David,
do not turn away the face of your anointed one.

Psalm 132:1–10

At the start of this chapter, I'd like to invite you into my study. Shift those commentaries to the side, ignore that stack of papers, and make yourself comfortable. The coffee will be ready in a few minutes.

I've invited you here because I want you to work with me through some of the steps I've worked through as I have read and studied this psalm. I want you to take some time to think about this passage with me.

First, did you notice something about the length of this psalm? It's the longest of the Songs of Ascents (I cover only the first ten verses in this chapter), and it's quite transparent as a pilgrim psalm. It's easy to see how Israelites going to the temple would sing these lines. In some ways, however, it's the most difficult of these psalms. It has unifying themes, as we'll see below, but in other respects it seems disjointed. How do the sections relate to one another?

Let's look a little more closely and see if we can answer our questions. As you read the psalm, did you notice that one person stands out in these verses? It's David. The psalm mentions him in verses 1, 10, 11, and 17. You find his name at the beginning, at the end, and with double emphasis in the middle.

Something else also comes to the forefront: a dwelling place for God. This appears in verses 5, 7, 8, 13, and 14. "David" and "a place for the LORD" are the main unifying themes of the psalm.

How else is the psalm unified? The first half is about David's oath to God (v. 2), while the second half is about God's oath to David (v. 11). Both the Lord and David are dedicated to a central place of worship for Israel. God has committed himself to manifesting his presence through the Davidic monarchy, and David has committed himself to seeking the presence of God, and a place for the ark of the covenant, at all costs.

What did it mean for David to seek God's presence? Isn't God everywhere? Yes, he is (see Ps. 139:7–11). But most of the time we go through life ignoring that fact. Israel was much the same. In the Old Testament, God provided special places where he would make it apparent to all that he was with his people. One of those places was the ark of the covenant, a unique chest that held the Ten Commandments. David committed to bringing the ark to the city of Jerusalem and putting it in a special place, a place where all Israel could come to worship.

The emphasis of the psalm is becoming clearer, but we need to ask some other questions. Who wrote this psalm? It's hard to say with absolute certainty, but I believe Solomon is a very likely candidate. Verses 8–10 are a quotation from his prayer of dedication for the temple (2 Chr. 6:41–42). But whether this is Solomon's voice, the voice of a later king, or the voices of Israelites who have returned from the Babylonian exile, the pilgrims who sang this psalm were seeking the presence and blessing of God through prayer, on the basis of God's dealings with David.

This brings us to our next question: How do we read this psalm as Christians? As a beautiful poem? A moral tale—that David worked hard for God and so should you? That's not entirely wrong, but it doesn't get to the heart of the passage. As Christians, we have to look at the links between what the psalmist wrote and what God has fully revealed in the person and work of Jesus.

In place of the temple in Jerusalem, God is now building his church (Eph. 2:21–22). You can see this theme in other psalms, especially Psalm 122. Like Zion, the church needs the presence of God. While these Old Testament believers sought it on the basis of God's dealings with David, we look to David's Son, the Lord Jesus Christ. Now bring those pieces together and you can see just how important this psalm is for you. You need the presence and blessing of God, and the way to get them is to seek them through Christ.

As we investigate this truth in the first ten verses of the psalm, we see that seeking God's presence is a matter of *priority* and of *prayer*.

A Matter of Priority

Knowing God, and experiencing his presence as he makes himself known through his own means, is the most important thing in the world. We can see this clearly in David's commitment. The psalm begins by asking the Lord to remember the dedication with which David pursued his calling to bring the ark to Jerusalem and see to it that God's people had a place to worship.

He was willing to endure hardships. He lost Uzzah on the first attempt to transport the ark. Uzzah reached out to steady the ark and was struck down (2 Sam. 6:5–11). Later, David told his son, Solomon, of his efforts to secure funding for the temple. "With great pains I have provided for the house of the LORD 100,000 talents of gold, a million talents of silver, and bronze and iron beyond weighing, for there is so much of it; timber and stone, too, I have provided. To these you must add" (1 Chr. 22:14). David sacrificed his time, his effort, and his resources.

He was willing to sacrifice personal comfort. His vow in verses 3–5 testifies to this. He would not go home to bed. He would not sleep until he accomplished the task. He did all this to see to it that men, women, and children had access to worship, access to God's dwelling place, where he made known his presence with the cloud of glory and where he displayed his grace and forgiveness at the altar of sacrifice.

Not only was David dedicated to this task, he led others to this commitment too. When you reach verse 6, do you notice a change? Do you see a shift in pronouns? In verses 1–5, the pronouns are singular: "he" and "I." But in verses 6 and 7 they're plural: "we" and "us." If you go back to the historical narrative of this occasion in 1 Chronicles 15, you'll see that David has inspired the entire nation to join him in his pursuit.

David led the people in the search for a place for the ark. He took great pains over the task, but others entered into his labors. David was the leader; he showed the way forward by dedicating himself to the job, by giving it his all, by establishing his priorities. But others, whom he had rallied to the cause, joined in. They wanted to worship too. He had shown them the importance of worship, and now it was their priority. This is what leaders are supposed to do.

What happened? When they were in Ephrathah, they heard about the ark. They went and found it in Jaar, or Kiriath-jearim. How did they react when they found it? "Let's go," they said. "Let's worship the Lord!" (see vv. 6–7). David had so inspired them that they were enthusiastic about taking the ark up to Jerusalem. His goal, dedication, and enthusiasm became theirs as well.

We see this same devotion in Christ. The Lord Jesus came to secure for us entrance into the presence of God. Have you ever thought about the commitment that took? In the prologue to his Gospel, John tells us that "the Word became flesh and dwelt among us, and we have seen his glory, glory as of the only Son from the Father, full of grace and truth" (John 1:14). John's wording is specific. Christ came, he says, and "tabernacled" among us. He came as the dwelling place of the glory of God. Paul taught this as well. In Christ we see the glory of God. "For God, who said, 'Let light shine out of darkness,' has shone in our hearts to give the light of the knowledge of the glory of God in the face of Jesus Christ" (2 Cor. 4:6).

Christ was also committed to going to the cross. As Luke unfolds the narrative of Jesus's life, he tells us that the Lord set his face to go to Jerusalem (Luke 9:51). We can see in Christ's face not only the glory of God but also the determination to accomplish his task. Jerusalem meant more suffering; it meant crucifixion. But that meant bringing many sons and daughters to glory (see Heb. 2:10)! For that, he was willing to endure all the hardship necessary.

David impoverished himself to build the temple. One hundred thousand talents of gold, a million talents of silver, and Solomon would have to add to it! But it was our Lord Jesus who gave up the riches of heaven to bring us to God. "For you know the grace of our Lord Jesus Christ, that though he was rich, yet for your sake he became poor, so that you by his poverty might become rich" (2 Cor. 8:9).

That kind of devotion from Christ calls for our devotion to him. Seeking God's presence and blessing in your life will involve hardship. It is never convenient or easy to follow Jesus. What did it cost David? Time, energy, and money. It will cost us no less.

But here's how so many of us try to work this out. We schedule our work time, family time, entertainment, hobbies, and so on, and then try to fit God into the bits that are left over. If we find that we don't have time to read the Bible, pray, and gather with God's people, that's unfortunate, but life's busy; that's just how it is.

No, it isn't. That's how we choose for life to be.

This week, you will probably use a planner, your phone, a kitchen calendar, or the back of an envelope to plan some part of your day or to jot down a "to do" list. Will you, in planning your week, prioritize God in your life?

An expert in time management stood before an audience and produced a large-mouthed gallon jar from under the table. He placed it on the table and then pulled out three fist-sized rocks and put them into the jar. "Is the jar full?" he asked. "Yes," the audience replied. He then pulled out a bucket of pebbles and poured them into the jar and shook them down into the crevices. "Is it full now?" The audience was starting to catch on and said "No." "Good," he replied. He then produced a bucket of sand and poured it into the jar. After that, he poured in water.

Then he asked, "What's the moral of the story?" Someone replied, "No matter how full your schedule is, if you try hard you can always fit in more stuff." "No!" the expert said. "The point of the story is that if you don't put in the big rocks first, you'll never get them into the jar!"[1]

What are the most important things in your life? If you don't put God first, you'll find that everything else crowds him out. Most of us are tired most of the time. We wonder why we're so exhausted. Is it not because we have failed first to rest? How are we keeping the Sabbath, the Lord's Day that God has given us for worship and rest? By not seeking the presence of God first, you rob yourself of the opportunity to have him set your priorities, calm your heart, and energize your walk and work.

A Matter of Prayer

Seeking God's presence is a matter of priority. But if we're determined to seek the Lord, how do we go about it? The answer is right here in the text. This psalm shows us that seeking God's presence is also a matter of prayer. The author casts the entire psalm in the mold of prayer. Verse 1 opens with a request for the Lord to remember David. But in verses 8–10 we come to specific requests.

The psalmist directly appeals to God to come. "Arise, O LORD, and go to your resting place" (v. 8). This is not the first time these words occur in the Bible. This prayer echoes the words of Moses. When the children of Israel marched from place to place in the wilderness, Moses would say, "'Arise, O LORD, and let your enemies be scattered, and let those who hate you flee before you.' And when [the ark] rested, he said, 'Return, O LORD, to the ten thousand thousands of Israel'" (Num. 10:35–36).

This was Solomon's prayer as the priests carried the ark of the covenant into the Most Holy Place (2 Chr. 6:41). For Solomon, this was a liturgy with a longing. It was a form he knew, but it expressed the desire of his heart.

The psalmist then asks for the priests to be clothed with righteousness and for the people to shout with joy (v. 9). When David brought the ark to Jerusalem and when Solomon dedicated the temple, the priests consecrated themselves, and the Levitical singers and musicians made sounds and songs of joy. Holiness and joy characterized their worship, and the glory of the Lord filled the house (1 Chr. 15:14–16; 2 Chr. 5:11–14).

Contrary to what the world tells us, holiness and joy go together. They are the appropriate responses to the presence of God. This is what our worship should be like. This is what our lives should be like. As we follow God's Word, as we continually receive cleansing from our sins through the blood of Jesus (see 1 John 1:7), we are pursuing the path of holiness and the way of happiness.

Do you cry out for God to fill the church with his presence? I think some of us are afraid to do that. Several years ago, I had lunch with a pastor friend. I knew that both of our churches were dedicated to praying for revival. But as we talked that day, we both admitted that we were scared. We were frightened. What would happen if God actually answered our prayers? What would it mean for us, for our churches, for our communities?

It's a fearful thing to pray "Arise, O LORD … you and the ark of your might!" This is the ark that led the armies of Israel, that defeated her enemies. When God arises and comes to his church with power, his enemies are laid low, sin is dealt with, and lives are changed.

This scares us so much because we are too comfortable in our sins and we don't want our lives disrupted. But what we fail to grasp is that such a movement of God will take us into the greatest experience of joy we can know this side of heaven!

Verses 8 and 9 provide us with content for our prayers. They tell us what we should be asking for. But how are we going to ask?

Put the pieces together. God's anointed one is praying. Who is this? I think it is Solomon or certainly one of the other Davidic kings.

What is he asking? "Hear my prayer. Do not turn my face away" (see v. 10).

Why is he praying this? "For the sake of your servant,

David. Hear my prayer based upon the regard you have for your chosen king."

Does this sound familiar? It's the way we pray when we conclude with the words "In Jesus's name, Amen." We're asking God to hear us based upon the regard he has for Christ.

Do you want God to hear and answer your prayers based on how well you obey him? If we want God to come to our churches and come to our lives with the fullness of his power, grace, and blessing, so that we are changed more and more into the image of his Son, we must plead with God in Jesus's name. We must call out for him to hear us for the sake of Christ who is now interceding at his right hand.

"Lord, don't turn us away. Don't leave us. Don't withdraw your hand so that we are left powerless and fruitless in our endeavor to serve you. Look upon us, the face of your chosen people, for Jesus's sake. Amen."

As we have seen, verses 8–10 are a quotation from Solomon's prayer of dedication at the temple. What happened when Solomon prayed this prayer?

> As soon as Solomon finished his prayer, fire came down from heaven and consumed the burnt offering and the sacrifices, and the glory of the LORD filled the temple. And the priests could not enter the house of the LORD, because the glory of the LORD filled the LORD's house. When all the people of Israel saw the fire come down and the glory of the LORD on the temple, they bowed down with their faces to the ground on the pavement

> and worshiped and gave thanks to the LORD, saying, "For he is good, for his steadfast love endures forever." (2 Chr. 7:1–3)

What resulted from Solomon's prayer for God's presence? Fire, glory, and worship! Let's ask for no less!

Reflect on These Points

1. *God's instructions in the Old Testament were often given through types. When reading the psalms, be sure to identify the unique elements of Old Testament revelation, like the ark of the covenant, so that you can make the appropriate New Testament links.*
2. *Are you determined to put first things first in your life? What will you do this week to prioritize the spiritual?*
3. *Do you pray for revival? What would happen if God came to your church?*
4. *To pray in Jesus's name is to come before the Father based on the merits of Christ and to seek for answers to our prayers that will glorify the name of Jesus. To pray in Christ's name is to prevail with God.*

Experiencing God's presence

The LORD swore to David a sure oath
from which he will not turn back:
"One of the sons of your body
I will set on your throne.
If your sons keep my covenant
and my testimonies that I shall teach them,
their sons also forever
shall sit on your throne."
For the LORD has chosen Zion;
he has desired it for his dwelling place:
"This is my resting place forever;
here I will dwell, for I have desired it.
I will abundantly bless her provisions;
I will satisfy her poor with bread.
Her priests I will clothe with salvation,
and her saints will shout for joy.
There I will make a horn to sprout for David;
I have prepared a lamp for my anointed.
His enemies I will clothe with shame,
but on him his crown will shine."

Psalm 132:11–18

I'm sure that, at one time or another, you have played hide-and-seek. I don't know about you, but I enjoy it more now as an adult than I did as a child. When you're a child playing the game, you don't want anyone to find you. You want to be the best hider. But as an adult, you want to see the joy and surprise on the child's face when he or she finally finds you. You can then scoop the child up in your arms, to squeals of delight, for a big hug. As an adult, you no longer want to be the best hider; you want to be found.

God wants to be found. In the previous chapter, we looked at the first half of Psalm 132 and its theme of seeking the presence of God in and through the person and work of Christ. You should make seeking God a matter of priority and a matter of prayer.

The first half of Psalm 132 describes David's efforts and Solomon's prayer. The second half of the psalm expounds God's promises and determination. We can see this in the "I will" statements that the Lord makes (vv. 11, 14, 15, 16, 17, 18). "I will ... I will ... I will ..." Do you get the impression that God is going to do something? God promises Israel, and through Israel he promises you and me, that he will be with us so that we will experience and enjoy his presence.

These repeated "I will" statements make the second half of this psalm an affirmation of assurance. Seeking God is not wasted effort. He is not having us play a cosmic game of cynical hide-and-seek. God assures us that he will be with us and bless us.

My Chosen King

That raises the question, "How will you and I know that the Lord is with us?" He gives us this assurance in two ways. First, he says, "I will be with you and bless you through my chosen king."

The second half of this psalm opens in verse 11 in a way that parallels the first. David swore an oath to God (v. 2). Now the Lord swears an oath to David. These verses take us back to 2 Samuel 7. David wanted to build a house for the Lord, but God would not allow it. David's reign had been one of warfare and hostility (see 1 Kings 5:3; 1 Chr. 22:8). Instead, the Lord promised to build a house for David, not with wood and stone, but with sons. God promised him a dynasty.

The Lord made this an unconditional promise. Note the emphasis in verse 11: the Lord "swore," he gave "a sure oath," one from which "he will not turn back." "One of the sons of your body I will set on your throne." God binds himself with the strongest affirmations. We read this same kind of language in God's covenant with Abraham in Hebrews 6:13–14: "For when God made a promise to Abraham, since he had no one greater by whom to swear, he swore by himself, saying, 'Surely I will bless you and multiply you.'" The language of verses 11 and 12 is strongly covenantal. It is oath-binding language.

The immediate fulfillment of this promise was Solomon. He was God's chosen one to build the temple. But verse 12 introduces us to a conditional promise. If David is to have sons who continue to reign over Israel, they must keep God's covenant and testimonies. Did this happen? Did the kings of Judah keep God's law? The tragic answer is "No." Some kings were godly, like Hezekiah, but some were also very wicked, especially Manasseh. Because of their sin, and especially because of the sin of Manasseh (see Jer. 15:4), God sent the

Babylonians as his instruments of judgment, and Judah went into exile.

The Psalms of Ascents were written over an extended period of time but were compiled during the period after the Babylonian exile. We can imagine Solomon singing this psalm, or perhaps even Asa or Hezekiah, before the great and awful destruction of Jerusalem. But how could Nehemiah sing this song? How do people sing words of assurance with any kind of joy or exuberance when they have experienced the trauma of exile?

The people of Israel sang this psalm because they knew that God is holy and just. The exile was not a mistake. They sang because the setbacks, the trauma, and the suffering were not the determining factors of God's Word or plan. They sang because the faithlessness of Judah's kings did not annul the faithfulness of God. The New Testament reinforces this truth. "What if some were unfaithful? Does their faithlessness nullify the faithfulness of God? By no means! Let God be true though every one were a liar" (Rom. 3:3–4). "If we are faithless, he remains faithful—for he cannot deny himself" (2 Tim. 2:13). The unshakable faithfulness of God sustained Israel and gave the people hope.

Because they knew of God's faithfulness, they sang with a faith that looked to the future. Faith must anticipate. "Now faith is the assurance of things hoped for, the conviction of things not seen" (Heb. 11:1). If faith didn't look to the future, it would leave us spiritually stagnant, wallowing in the present as if it were the ultimate reality.

It was this forward-looking faith that gave Israel hope. Is God's promise in verse 11 just about Solomon? Was he the ultimate and final fulfillment? No! On the day of Pentecost, Peter preached to Jews gathered in Jerusalem from all over the ancient world, Jews who were still experiencing the aftershocks of exile and who had come together to celebrate one of the pilgrim feasts. Peter proclaimed that David,

> being therefore a prophet, and knowing that God had sworn with an oath to him that he would set one of his descendants on his throne, ... foresaw and spoke about the resurrection of the Christ, that he was not abandoned to Hades, nor did his flesh see corruption. This Jesus God raised up, and of that we all are witnesses. (Acts 2:30–32)

Peter preached the gospel of the kingdom. Christ's death and resurrection bring believers under his rule, where he reigns in righteousness, peace, and joy. We are not waiting for a Messianic king in the future. We have one now! This is the bedrock guarantee that God is with us.

If God guarantees us his presence through the chosen King, how do we experience that, since his King is in heaven and not on earth? The answer lies in what God has exalted Christ to do. He is at the Father's right hand to give us the Holy Spirit. Jesus promised in John 14:15–31 that he would not leave us; he would send the Spirit.

We enjoy the presence of God through his Word. In it, the Holy Spirit speaks to us. We enjoy it through pursuing holiness. As we seek to obey God's law, we are striving not to grieve the Spirit (Eph. 4:30). As we submit to the Lordship of Christ, and as we believe his gospel more and more, he continues to fill us with the Spirit. By trusting in Christ, we receive more and more of the Spirit's influence and power in our lives (see Gal. 3:5). We pray to be filled with the Spirit (Eph. 5:18).

When we begin to ask "Where is God? Where is he in my marriage? Where is he in my work, my family, my studies?", the answer is "He is with me. He lives in me by his Spirit, and I am to approach my marriage, my career, my schoolwork, everything I do, as a Spirit-filled believer." When the Lord seems far away, ask yourself, "Am I believing what he has done for me in Christ, am I submitting to the power of the Spirit, and am I praying for the filling of the Spirit?"

Perhaps you wonder if God is with you at all. You often ask yourself, "Am I really a Christian?" If that's the question on your mind, it is Jesus you need. God has exalted him as King because he has accepted his work on the cross as the payment for sin's penalty. If you will accept that truth about King Jesus, you will be saved.

Jonathan Edwards was perhaps the greatest theologian America has ever produced, but he was not always a Christian. As he looked back upon his life, he believed that God's quickening work began in his heart as he meditated on 1 Timothy 1:17: "To the King of the ages, immortal, invisible, the only God, be honor and glory forever and ever. Amen."[1] It was this great King, this immortal and glorious God, whom he wanted to know.

Do you want to know this great King? Then turn your heart toward heaven and ask Christ to save you. Tell him that you will bow to the scepter of King Jesus. Tell him that you will be his loyal subject.

My Chosen Place

God is with us through the reigning Lordship of his chosen King. But the text emphasizes a second point: God assures us of his presence and blessing in his chosen place.

In the closing verses of this psalm, the focus shifts back to Zion. God has chosen her: there's no doubt about it. This is the city he wants as his own. Here he will dwell, here he will manifest his presence, here he will gather his people to worship, and here he will pour out his blessing, the riches and the fullness of his redemptive grace. When you think about Zion, don't confine your mental conceptions to a city of buildings, houses, and shops. The city of Zion is a community, a covenant community, the Old Testament church, the assembly of the people of God.

The psalmist emphasizes three things about this community of God's people. First, the Lord initiates the relationship with his people. Zion is chosen and desired (vv. 13–14). What is true of the place is true of the people. God loves his people. He desires and delights in them as the objects of his grace.

Isn't this the New Testament's description of the church? The

Lord did not choose the university, government, industry—or even the family, as important as it is. He has set aside a body of believers, an assembly of saints, to be his chosen dwelling place.

What is true for the church corporately is true for her members individually. God chose us in Christ before the foundation of the world (Eph. 1:4). God instigates this relationship. That's the point behind the doctrine of election. If you're a believer in Christ, it's because God started the work. You can be certain that he'll finish what he has begun (Phil. 1:6). The doctrine of election doesn't rob us of assurance; it provides a foundation for it.

Never look at the doctrine of election as cold and sterile. Never think of God's choice of a people as something remote and unfeeling, as though he were sitting on his throne with a marker, ticking off one for heaven and one for hell. That's not the view Scripture gives us. We should always look at God's election in terms of love and delight.

The second thing the psalmist emphasizes about this community of God's people is that God provides for her (vv. 15–16). The Lord promises material blessings. He will bless her with provisions and see that she has an ample supply of food and water. The poor need not worry; they will have food too.

What God promised here, David and Solomon provided. When David brought the ark to Jerusalem, he distributed food to the people (2 Sam. 6:18–19). When Solomon dedicated the temple, he held a great feast (1 Kings 8:65–66; 2 Chr. 7:8–10).

The Lord also promised spiritual blessings. Verse 16 is a direct answer to the prayer of verse 9. Israel's priests will be clothed with salvation. With the priests under divine protection, they can carry out their duties in the temple, pointing again and again to the need for sacrifice and cleansing. In this context, the saints shout with joy. God will provide for their spiritual needs. Not only will they have full stomachs, they will also have full hearts!

If we bring these two aspects together, what we see God doing is this: he's caring for his people as whole people. They are neither disembodied spirits nor spiritless bodies. They are body and soul, and God fully provides for them.

We see this same pattern in the New Testament. In Acts 6, the church distributed food to the poor widows, but they also needed men to minister the Word and prayer. As the church, we must never neglect people as people, people as body and soul. How we interact with the physical needs of others demonstrates our attitude toward them. If a cold, hungry person comes to us and we say, "Be warm, be filled, and be on your way" without seeking to feed and clothe him or her, how do we demonstrate the love of Jesus Christ? Are we showing that we have a living faith in him? (See James 2:14–17.)

However, if we become concerned *only* with the physical needs of others and neglect to feed them the Word of God and clothe them with the garments of salvation, what ultimate good have we done? We must look out for the needs of people, *especially* the need they have for salvation through Jesus Christ.

Caring for people body and soul cannot be an either/or proposition. It must be both/and. God calls for us to be concerned for the whole person. For this reason, he has given both deacons and elders to the church. Each office has a specific focus, but just because the elders have the spiritual oversight of the church, that doesn't mean that the office of the deacon is any less spiritual. Without both offices functioning in complete dependence upon the Lord, the work of the church will become unbalanced.

As the church seeks to follow her God-given responsibility, she will experience God's grace and help to follow his directives. And as we experience that kind of grace from the Lord, we will know that he is with us. God is concerned to make his presence known through the full-orbed ministry of the body of Christ.

The triumph of the king is the third and final aspect of this chosen city (vv. 17–18). God not only initiates the relationship with his people and provides for them, he also rules over them. In the closing verses, the psalm brings us back full circle to David—more precisely, to David's son, whom God will set on his throne in Jerusalem. It's impossible to disentangle David and Zion. The fortunes of each are bound up with the other. God chose his king, and he chose the place for him to reign. The political capital of Israel was her spiritual capital as well.

As you study verses 17 and 18, you'll see that God is going

to do several things for this son of David. First, he will cause a horn to sprout. A well-known symbol of strength, the horn that sprouts for David is none other than Jesus himself. When Mary, the mother of Jesus, sang of God's fulfilled promises, she included this feature. In the birth of her son, the Lord had "raised up a horn of salvation for us in the house of his servant David" (Luke 1:69).

Second, he will give him a lamp to illumine. Several times in the Old Testament, the lamp refers to the light of God that shines through the Davidic line of kings. God promised that David would always have a light to shine (1 Kings 11:36; 15:4; 2 Kings 8:19; 2 Chr. 21:7). This is a restatement of the covenant promise made in verse 11.

Third, he will give him a crown to shine. Here's the promise of a resplendent kingship, a dazzling reign, a majestic monarchy.

What will all this mean for his enemies? They will be clothed with shame. In spite of all the blessings that God promises through this king, he will still have enemies. People will rebel against his rule. They will reject him to their own shame. The imagery is strong. Shame will cover the rebels. This is a euphemistic way of saying that God will judge them.

Reading this psalm from the perspective of the New Testament, we as Christians identify Zion then with the church now. The church is where Christ rules as in no other place. It's God's chosen dwelling place, where we experience his presence. If we reject the church, we reject Christ; we reject the presence of God with his people.

Some people maintain that they can worship God in nature just as well as they can in church, but that's impossible. Is God present when you walk through a forest? Absolutely! Can you pray, rejoice in, and admire the beauty of his creation? Certainly! But if you do this to the exclusion of the church, your worship will be skewed and ultimately perverted. God has chosen a place that he delights in, a place where he meets the needs of his people, a place unlike any other where he displays the Kingship of Jesus, and that place is the church.

Psalm 87:2 expresses it this way: "The LORD loves the gates of Zion more than all the dwelling places of Jacob." Does God love the dwelling places of Jacob? Absolutely! He loves all his people in all places at all times. But he loves the gates of Zion even more! He loves not just individuals; he loves his covenant community as well. We worship God in private, with our families, in our small groups, in our Bible studies. All these should draw out our hearts to love and rejoice in the Lord. But something special happens when God's people gather to worship. We can experience some means of grace, such as preaching and the sacraments, only as a gathered body.

The Lord tells us to seek him because he wants us to experience the thrill and joy of discovery. But he also wants to assure us that he is with us so that we don't despair and think our search is in vain. In this Song of Ascents, we hear those bass notes of assurance and the melody of grace.

The joy of discovering God's presence comes in the person of Christ as the exalted King of his church. And it comes in the church as the place God has chosen to bless.

Will you have Christ? Will you have his church?

Reflect on These Points

1. *Since the Lord wants us to find him, seeking him is always profitable. It is never a waste of time. "For thus says the LORD, who created the heavens [he is God], who formed the earth and made it [he established it; he did not create it empty, he formed it to be inhabited!]: 'I am the LORD, and there is no other. I did not speak in secret, in a land of darkness; I did not say to the offspring of Jacob, "Seek me in vain." I the LORD speak the truth; I declare what is right'" (Isa. 45:18–19).*
2. *When you feel most alone, God is still with you.*
3. *Christ is not waiting to become King when he returns. He is now enthroned at the Father's right hand as King over all.*
4. *You can rely upon God's promises. He has committed himself to you.*

The beauty of unity

Behold, how good and pleasant it is
when brothers dwell in unity!
It is like the precious oil on the head,
running down on the beard,
on the beard of Aaron,
running down on the collar of his robes!
It is like the dew of Hermon,
which falls on the mountains of Zion!
For there the LORD has commanded the blessing,
life forevermore.

Psalm 133

"To live above with the saints we love, / Oh that will be glory. / But to live below with the saints we know, / Well, that's another story."[1] We can laugh at those lines, but their humor reflects a sad reality. Christians are often not united.

The Bible tells the story of divided brothers, divided families, divided friends, and divided churches. A quick survey of biblical history reveals how sin ripped apart relationships. Cain and Abel. Abraham and Lot. Isaac and Ishmael. Jacob and Esau. Joseph and his brothers. Solomon and Adonijah. Israel and Judah. Jesus and Judas. The church at Corinth. The church at Philippi.

But the Bible also tells the story of unity through redemption: Joseph and his brothers were reunited in Egypt and later, as a nation, redeemed from bondage. Judah and Israel were divided and exiled, yet God's people returned to the land of promise to reunite, rebuild, and await the coming of the Messiah.

The church has struggled and still struggles with divisions, but on the final day of redemption, Christ will return and take us to his New Jerusalem, the new Zion, for the great and final pilgrim feast, the marriage supper of the Lamb (Rev. 19:9). In heaven, the people of God will unite, never to divide again. To dwell above with saints I love, for me that will be glory! But to dwell below with saints I know—what will speak to that?

To Israel suffering the effects of the divided kingdom and exile, and to the church awaiting the return of Christ, Psalm 133 speaks with a clear voice about the beauty, the desirability, and hence the necessity, of God's people striving for unity.

God's Marketing Plan

The text begins with the word "Behold." This is the red, flashing beacon of the Old Testament. "Behold" grabs you by the shoulders, looks you in the eye, and says, "You'd better listen to this! What I'm about to tell you is very important. It is good for brothers to live in unity."

I think of this psalm as God's marketing plan for unity. That may not sound very spiritual, but think about it for a moment. How does a business market its products? It makes them desirable. Restaurants do this all the time. Their ads say things like, "Plump, juicy chicken. Crispy, golden crust. The perfect blend of seasonings." The ad never says, "Would you like some chicken?" It doesn't have to ask. The description is all the invitation you need.

Much of this brief psalm describes what unity among God's people is like. If you're a believer and you hear this description, the Lord doesn't have to ask, "Would you like to be united?" Your heart should immediately respond, "What this passage describes is exactly what I want!"

Unity Equals Togetherness

As you look at God's description more closely, you'll see that, in its essence, unity is togetherness. A very wooden, literal translation of verse 1 would read this way: "Behold, how good and how pleasant to dwell, brothers, even together." Togetherness lies at the heart of unity.

The Israelites who sang this pilgrim psalm were traveling together to the same place, Zion. They were going to join together in the same worship. They shared the same history and doctrine. And, as they marched up to Zion, they were united in their goals and aspirations. But at an even deeper level, they shared a common ancestry. They were brothers, a family, a clan. They shared the same bloodline and the same DNA.

Unity is more than a common interest. People join clubs and organizations because they share a hobby, a vocation, or enjoy the same sport. But the togetherness described in our passage is the unity of a common bond in Christ.

Unity equals togetherness, and that's what makes it so good and pleasing. David, the author of this psalm, states this truth in plain language. Pay attention to this! When brothers are together, their unity has God's seal of approval. It's good. And unity will give you a sense of satisfaction and enjoyment. It's pleasant.

David also illustrates his statement. He compares unity to the fragrant anointing oil that Moses poured on Aaron when he became high priest, and to the dew of Hermon that falls so heavily that it soaks the ground. Fragrant and refreshing! What a beautiful picture!

But let's be honest. It's easy to hold out unity as an ideal. It's not difficult to attend gatherings that represent the broader Christian community, or conferences made up of a broad denominational spectrum. But it is difficult to maintain unity as a practice. It's easy to talk about unity and the glory of heaven. But to dwell below with the saints I know, well, that's another story.

Self-centeredness keeps us from striving harder to achieve unity. We can't see the beauty of unity because we can't get our eyes off ourselves and our agendas. The last time you were in a conflict with someone, were you more interested in promoting the joy of unity that God presents here, or in justifying yourself?

If, in its essence, unity is togetherness, being together promotes unity. Believers should gather together for worship (Heb. 10:25). To promote unity on the Lord's Day, though, Christians should be together during the week too. Isn't this the pattern we see in the early church?

> And they devoted themselves to the apostles' teaching and the fellowship, to the breaking of bread and the

> prayers ... And all who believed were together and had all things in common ... And day by day, attending the temple together and breaking bread in their homes, they received their food with glad and generous hearts, praising God and having favor with all the people. And the Lord added to their number day by day those who were being saved. (Acts 2:42–47)

How well do we reflect that kind of togetherness?

If you confuse hospitality with entertaining, you will likely hinder togetherness. Entertaining can be fun. There's nothing wrong with it. But if we're not careful, entertaining can become a production that says, "Look what I can do." Hospitality, however, says, "Share my home, share my food, share my time, share my thoughts, share my faith, share my joy."

The summer I graduated from high school, I traveled with a Christian ministry team. My team members and I were in about fifty homes in ten weeks. Some homes were palatial. Others were pitiful. I remember one home in particular where the mother was struggling to feed her own family and yet wanted to share what little they had with others to minister to the body of Christ. Will you open your heart and your home like that to promote the togetherness of God's people?

The Origins of Unity

Psalm 133 tells us not only what unity is like, but also where unity originates. You may read this passage and conclude that it has nothing to say about the origins of unity, but look closely.

Do you remember what your English teacher taught you about poetry? Read between the lines. That doesn't mean read into the text something that isn't there. It means to read out of the text the fullness of the meaning that's encapsulated in the imagery. Two images stand at the heart of this psalm: the anointing of Aaron and the dew of Hermon.

God gave instructions for anointing Aaron in Exodus 29, and you can read about the actual events of his consecration in Leviticus 8. Moses anointed Aaron at the command of God. And though Moses was the instrument, it was the Lord himself who set apart Aaron for the role of high priest. The anointing ultimately came from God.

Next, David mentions the dew of Hermon. Evidently proverbial in ancient Israel, the dew of Hermon settled on the mountain every evening because it was far to the north and, due to its great height, experienced much cooler temperatures at night. While that's the natural explanation for its heavy dew, we know that dew ultimately comes from God.

Finally, notice how David describes the oil and the dew. He uses a key word that means "to run down." It occurs three times in this brief psalm. You see it in verse 2: the oil is "running down" on Aaron's beard; it's "running down" on his collar. It occurs in verse 3 as well. The ESV translates it as "which falls," but it's the very same word. The dew of Hermon is *running down* on the mountains of Zion!

Now, put yourself in the sandals of an Israelite walking to the feast. You're going *up* to Jerusalem. What are you singing? A Song of Ascents, a song of going up! Surely those who sang this psalm did not miss the contrasting play on words. *We're going up, up, up, and the blessing is coming down, down, down.*

When the Jews assembled to worship, when they were all together in Zion, who was it that sent the blessing? The Lord himself commanded it (v. 3)!

Being together promotes unity, but unity originates with God. Unity reflects the nature of God. Before time and space existed, God was united in himself in perfect harmony, love, and fellowship as Father, Son, and Holy Spirit.

Unity reflects the relationship of Christ and his people. Jesus expresses both these truths in his High Priestly prayer of John 17. The One anointed by God prays,

> I do not ask for these only, but also for those who will believe in me through their word, that they may all be one, just as you, Father, are in me, and I in you, that they also may be in us, so that the world may believe that you have sent me. The glory that you have given me I have given to them, that they may be one even as we are one, I in them and you in me, that they may become perfectly one, so that the world may know that you sent me and loved them even as you loved me. (John 17:20–23)

This prayer of Jesus describes part of the work that he came to accomplish to reunite those divided by sin. He came to reconcile us to God by the blood of his cross (Col. 1:20). Ours was the worst breach of unity. Christ died to bring us into the family of God. The gospel means that we belong together.

Every summer, in early July, MacRae Meadow on Grandfather Mountain is awash in a sea of colorful tents and tartans as those of Scottish descent gather in the mountains of western North Carolina for the Grandfather Mountain Highland Games, the largest gathering of Scottish clans in the world. Tens of thousands come to the meadow because of a common interest in Highland heritage and culture. But the MacDonalds don't find their identity at the Ross tent. The MacLarens are not the House of Gordon. When you go to your clan tent, that's the one place in the meadow where, like no other, you belong. If you're a believer in Christ, the gospel has brought you into the family, the clan, of the church. That's the place where, like no other, you belong.

Jesus Christ came to unite Jew and Gentile in his body, the church, by breaking down the barrier that divided us (Eph. 2:11–15). When Christ returns, all his people, both living and dead, will be caught up together with him in the clouds (1 Thes. 4:16–17).

When John saw the New Jerusalem coming down from God (Rev. 21), he described one Bride, the wife of the Lamb, one city with twelve gates (for the tribes of Israel) and twelve foundations (for the twelve apostles), and one united people of God.

The unity of God's people is gospel unity, and that's why

disunity is so tragic. It's a failure to live out the implications of the work of Christ.

What Unity Brings

If we are willing to seek unity among ourselves by living out the gospel, what will that bring to the church? Let's go back to verse 2 and unpack the imagery a little more.

If unity is like anointing oil, then it produces an atmosphere of sweetness. Exodus 30:22–33 gives a list of the ingredients for compounding the special oil used to anoint the priests. It was made from liquid myrrh, cinnamon, aromatic cane, and cassia. This would have had a fragrant, even pungent, pleasant odor. Everyone who was near could have smelled it because David describes an abundance of oil. It ran down over Aaron's head, down his beard, and onto his robe.

The church experienced this kind of sweet atmosphere of unity in the book of Acts. Paul encourages unity in the worship at Corinth so that the church will have a testimony to those who hear the Word of God from them, a testimony that will cause people to confess "God is really among you" (1 Cor. 14:25).

Unity will make your church smell good. When visitors attend your assembly, can they sense that you are one in Christ? Is your unity such that people are compelled to say, "God is really among you"?

Unity not only brings an atmosphere of sweetness, it also brings life. The dew of Hermon kept the area lush and green. How different that northern region was from dry Judea. Unity is like an abundance of water in an arid wilderness. It provides refreshment, spiritual strength, power, and health to the church.

It will also give believers a taste of heaven on earth. In his final comment, David remarks that in Zion, where brothers are gathered, God commands the blessing of life forevermore. What does it mean for God to command his blessing? He speaks his word to bless, and it happens. It is as though the many blessings he gives to his people stand before him as his servants. He says to one, "Go." And it goes. To another, "Do this." And it does it.

When the church is united, God says, "Let there be life in that place." Disunity grieves the Holy Spirit. It drives away his blessing and power. It robs us of effective witness. It destroys our testimony. Unity and disunity have eternal consequences!

Why does the psalm highlight the blessing of eternal life? Why this blessing from unity and not some other? In Zion, God has commanded life forevermore because Zion is a picture of the dwelling place of God—heaven. It is good and pleasant for brothers to dwell in unity in Zion because that is a picture of heaven on earth. When the people of God are united, it's a taste of heaven on earth. A united church below experiences the joy of heaven above.

Will you dedicate yourself to the unity of the church? Will you say to the Lord, "Father, let me never bring harm or division to your body. Use me as your instrument to bring fragrant, life-giving unity to the body of believers where I worship."

If you're willing to pray that, how can you promote the unity of the church? Begin by drinking deeply at the well of the gospel. Meditate on the unity of the Godhead and your union with Christ, and therefore your union with every believer.

Pray for an open heart and an understanding mind so that you can discern what is of primary importance, so that you can reach out with love even to those with whom you differ.

Be willing to put aside differences on secondary issues. Give people the Christian liberty you want for yourself.

Spend time together, read the Bible together, pray together.

Finally, celebrate your oneness with Christ and his body by gathering regularly to hear the Word of God preached and to celebrate the Lord's Supper. If you approach biblical unity with these attitudes, you'll discover that your church smells good and is the most refreshing place you know!

Reflect on These Points

1. *Are you united with the people in your church? Are you involved in a conflict that needs resolution? God has given you a way to pursue restoration. Follow the biblical steps of Matthew 18:15–20.*
2. *Are your relationships with other believers a marketing plan for Christian unity?*
3. *What can you do this week to promote togetherness with the people of your church?*
4. *Oil in the Bible is sometimes a picture of the Holy Spirit. How does the Spirit promote unity in the church?*

Blessing given and received

Come, bless the Lord, *all you servants of the* Lord,
who stand by night in the house of the Lord!
Lift up your hands to the holy place
and bless the Lord!
May the Lord *bless you from Zion,*
he who made heaven and earth!

Psalm 134

The Psalms of Ascents stirred the hearts and informed the minds of the Israelites who journeyed to Jerusalem to worship at the annual feasts of Passover, Pentecost, and Tabernacles.

As we've studied these psalms, we've traveled a long, difficult, and dangerous journey. Our trip began in hostile territory, in places like Meshech and Kedar (Ps. 120). The hills that lay between our hometown and Jerusalem loomed large, with threats of bandits and rough terrain (Ps. 121). But that city, bound firmly together, the seat of David's reign, has, all along, been a worthwhile destination (Ps. 122).

We've looked to the Lord for our help just as a servant looks to his or her master (Ps. 123), and we've realized that if the Lord had not been on our side, the journey would never have been possible (Ps. 124).

Zion, the city to which we've been marching, has provided for us an example of stability (Ps. 125) and a hope for renewal (Ps. 126).

Our pilgrimage has given us the opportunity to search our

hearts about our work and home (Ps. 127), express our hopes and hardships (Ps. 128 and 129), and lament our sins (Ps. 130). The Lord has taught us to calm down (Ps. 131) and look up (Ps. 132)!

When we made it to the city and discovered our brothers and sisters from all over the land, oh, how wonderful that was! The atmosphere even smelled good! It was refreshing! In Zion, God poured out the blessing of life forevermore (Ps. 133)!

Now it's time to return to our villages and towns. The feast is over. The sun is sinking behind the Judean hills. It's time to get back to building houses, keeping cities, plowing fields, and raising families.

But before we leave Jerusalem, we need to do one last thing. We turn and cry out to the temple servants, "Bless the LORD!" To which they reply, "The LORD bless you!" What a fitting conclusion to a pilgrim's worship!

The Lord wraps up this little psalm in that word "bless." This word gets right to the heart of our worship. Blessing isn't all that happens in worship, but it defines the broader context. In worship, blessing flows to and from the Lord.

Bless the Lord!

Let's begin by noting that blessing characterizes our relationship to the Lord in worship. We can sum up the message of verses 1 and 2 in the command "Bless the LORD."

As dusk falls and the temple workers change shifts, the pilgrims gather around Mount Zion and call to those working in the temple precincts, "Come, bless the LORD, all you servants of the LORD, who stand by night in the house of the LORD!" (v. 1).

These servants are obviously Levites. Various guilds of Levitical workers served at the temple. While Aaron's sons served as the priests, the descendants of Gershon, Kohath, and Merari had responsibilities for the actual equipment and materials needed for the temple to function properly (see Num. 3).

The particular servants the psalmist refers to "stand by night in the house of the LORD." Some Levitical singers ministered during the night (1 Chr. 9:33), while others policed the temple grounds and saw to it that everything was ready for the next day's worship to begin with the early morning sacrifice. These workers performed their duties out of the limelight, yet their jobs were very important. The tasks were unseen but not insignificant.

What service did they carry out during the night? The pilgrims call on these Levites to serve the Lord by lifting their hands to the holy place and blessing him. To lift one's hands in worship and prayer was a common posture during Old Testament times. Worshipers would lift their hands and stretch them out as a gesture toward God, a physical expression of directing their energies, thoughts, and emotions toward the Lord.

It also signified the worshiper's expectation of receiving an answer from the Lord. A person made a request of God and then reached out his or her hands to receive the answer. To lift your hands in worship and prayer, then, was an act of devotion and of expectation. For example, we read in Psalm 28:1–2,

> To you, O LORD, I call;
>   my rock, be not deaf to me,

lest, if you be silent to me,
  I become like those who go down to the pit.
Hear the voice of my pleas for mercy,
  when I cry to you for help,
when I lift up my hands
  toward your most holy sanctuary.

When the pilgrims ask the Levites to lift their hands to the holy place, they are asking them to worship by faith as they bless the Lord.

It's an important Bible study tip to know that the same word can have different meanings. For example, in English the word "bank" can mean a financial institution or the sloping land beside a river. The context determines the meaning. Hopefully, you're sensitive to that context and don't dig into the bank of a river to deposit your money!

Similarly, the word "bless" has several different meanings in the Old Testament. In verses 1 and 2, it means "to praise." To bless God is to recount the greatness and the grandeur of his person and attributes; it's to thank him for who he is and for all that he has done for us. We praise God when we express our reverence for him and our gratitude to him for all things. The Levites are to make their nightly rounds and worship God with hearts and mouths full of praise and thanksgiving.

While the pilgrims encourage this kind of godly worship, any faithful Israelite who took the time to think about it would realize that no Levite could do this perfectly. While the Levites represented the people in their worship and did many important and essential things in and for worship, at the end of the day they were mere men and suffered from all the foibles of fallen, sinful creatures. So every faithful Israelite who called on the Levites to worship the Lord did so with a note of anticipation.

The ancient pilgrims anticipated a servant of the Lord whose worship would be flawless. They anticipated a priesthood unlike the Levites, one anchored in the annals of covenant history—a priest forever after the order of Melchizedek (Ps. 110:4), yet a priesthood with all the freshness and spiritual vitality of one who lives forever (Heb. 5:6; 7:3, 17, 21). They worshiped in anticipation of the coming of the Lord Jesus Christ.

The Lord Jesus is the true Priest who worships God. It was Christ who lifted his holy hands on the cross and blessed the Lord when he offered up himself as the perfect sacrifice for our sins. It's important for us to see the life and sacrifice of Christ as acts of worship, because throughout his entire life Jesus loved the Lord his God with all his heart, mind, soul, and strength. It's only because Christ has worshiped God perfectly that you and I can worship him at all.

Because Christ is the perfect and everlasting Priest, he brings all believers into the priesthood, with direct access to God (1 Peter 2:9). Now that Christ has lifted his hands in holiness, faith, and praise, you and I are called to this same kind of service.

The Lord has brought us into the priesthood of believers not primarily for our benefit, but for his. Salvation is about forgiveness, righteousness, peace in our hearts, and a home in heaven. But if that is all salvation is to you, you have a very man-centered view of the work of Christ. Salvation is about God. He's the One we bless. We lift our hands to him. The cross is about God. Salvation is about taking wicked, sinful, rebellious people like you and me and making us the Lord's servants, so that he gets the service of worship, praise, and glory. Any outlook on the Christian life less than that is sub-biblical. The work of Christ is not about giving us fulfilled lives. That is, at best, the byproduct of the gospel. It's not the gospel or the primary purpose of the gospel. The gospel is all about God.

All our service is for God, whether it's notable or not. Think about all the work that takes place at night, all the jobs that are virtually unseen but absolutely vital. Employees at electric plants, policemen and emergency workers, those who clean the emergency room and operating theaters at the hospital, people driving snow plows—all work through the night to keep our lives running smoothly during the day. Few people see these workers, but could any of us do without them?

How do you look at your service for the Lord? You may feel like a lab rat running the maze of cubicles at work. Or your day may consist of changing diapers and cleaning up the latest mishap. Your work for the Lord may not be glamorous. Few people may notice it. You may receive little or no thanks. But that doesn't mean that what you do to serve the Lord is unimportant to him. Every act offered in praise to God for the glory of God is significant.

What's the most important light in your house? One preacher used to say that it's not the chandelier in the dining room, though that may look impressive. The most important light is the one in the back hallway that keeps you from stumbling when you get up at night. No matter how small your role in the kingdom may seem, it is not trivial. You have the unparalleled privilege of praising the Lord with your words and actions!

The Lord Bless You!

We bless God when we worship. That's the thrust of verses 1 and 2. In verse 3, the Levites reply. The pilgrims have issued a call to worship: "Come, bless the LORD." Now the Levites respond with a benediction.

The first words of verse 3 are identical to the Aaronic blessing in Numbers 6:24–26: "The LORD bless you and keep you; the LORD make his face to shine upon you and be gracious to you; the LORD lift up his countenance upon you and give you peace." This archetypal blessing is fundamentally covenantal in character. After the high priest offered a sacrifice, he raised his hands and conveyed the blessing of God's covenant promises to the people.

We see this same pattern in the ministry of the Lord Jesus. After his crucifixion and resurrection, he led his disciples out to the Mount of Olives and, just before he ascended into heaven, he lifted up his hands and blessed them (Luke 24:50). The indication is clear from the Old Testament and the New—

every covenant blessing flows from the blood of the sacrifice. On the cross, Christ took the curse of the covenant on himself so that all the benefits of the covenant might flow to us.

Now, based on the Aaronic blessing, the Levites (probably lifting up their hands) pronounce this benediction: "May the LORD bless you from Zion, he who made heaven and earth" (v. 3)! The "you" is not plural. It's not, as we Southerners say, "Y'all." It's you the individual. This is a personal message.

This benediction is not a prayer; it's a pronouncement. In pronouncing the benediction, the Levites were passing on the blessings of the covenant that God had made with Abraham, Isaac, and Jacob. All Abraham's descendants, both physical and spiritual, are entitled to these blessings. It is the responsibility of those ordained to the task to pass them on.[1]

The Lord has the power to send down these blessings because he is the One who made heaven and earth (see Ps. 124:8). The end of the psalm underscores his creative power, his sheer, raw ability. At his disposal are the resources of omnipotence.

He is the God of creation, the God of natural revelation, the God of common grace, but he has only one source of blessing. The Lord blesses his pilgrims from Zion. Zion was the Old Testament stage for the drama of redemption, the place where men enacted the gospel day after day with sacrifices and ceremonies.

The blessings that come to God's people come from Zion, but Mount Zion in Jerusalem was a pattern for something far greater. As the place of sacrifice, Zion points to the cross. As the locale of the temple, Zion points to the church and to the ultimate dwelling place of God—heaven itself.

When the Levites pronounce this benediction, they're giving a blessing that comes from heaven with all the omnipotent power of the Creator behind it.

In Presbyterian churches, it is the custom at a minister's ordination that he takes no part in the service until the end. At that point, another minister leads him into the pulpit to pronounce the benediction. His first task and privilege as a minister of the New Covenant is to pass on the blessings of that covenant to the people. Then, week by week, the pastor gives the blessing of the Lord to his congregation.

How do you respond to the benediction? For some, it's like the closing credits of a movie. The action is over. These are just the details to wrap up things.

In some churches, people bow their heads during the benediction because it seems like a prayer for blessing, but it's not. It's a pronouncement of God's intention to bless his people. It's proper to look up and receive the blessing of God, to hear his words and promises of grace, and embrace them by faith. The benediction is not our cue that the pastor has finally finished. It's our opportunity to share with our gathered brothers and sisters all the good benefits the Lord has for us. It's our opportunity to receive his grace and strength and to take them with us on our pilgrim journey.

Do you know you're blessed? You may look at your bank account or your retirement account and feel cursed. You may look at conflicts in your family and wonder how God could possibly be doing anything good in your life. For you, the benediction is just a bunch of pious but empty words that ministers are supposed to say.

The pastor gives the benediction, but you must receive it. Trust God for the blessings of the covenant and they will be yours. Take the blessing with you for your week. Take it for those times you feel more doom and discouragement than you do goodness and grace. Take God's blessing for the times when you're overwhelmed and frustrated. Take it for those times when you doubt the Lord's good purposes for your life.

In those moments when you think God is against you, remember that you have been blessed. Christ Jesus lifts up his holy hands, prays for you (Heb. 7:25), and pronounces a benediction on you. You are blessed and you remain blessed in him. Therefore every bit of wisdom that you need, every ounce of strength you need, every glimmer of faith you need, is available to you.

When you look around and see the mighty power of God in creation, when you look at the trees and understand that no one has the power to make a tree, when you look at a sunset and realize that no artist could paint it, that should give you the confidence that you can hope in God for anything. He has made heaven and earth. What do you need from the Lord right now? He has the ability to meet that need.

He's not only able, he's also willing. Paul wrote in Romans 8:32, "He who did not spare his own Son but gave him up for us all, how will he not also with him graciously give us all things?" If he gave Christ for you, will he withhold any good thing from you that Christ has purchased?

With the blessing given and received, we make our way onto the road that leads home. We're content because we know another festival will come. We'll be back to celebrate the Feast of Tabernacles or Passover again. And one day, one glorious day, our village, our home, and Zion will be one. The blessing pronounced upon us will come to full fruition. We'll sit down at the wedding feast of the Lamb. We'll raise our hands and bless the Lord!

Reflect on These Points

1. *In what ways can you relate the Psalms of Ascents to your own Christian pilgrimage?*
2. *When we bless the Lord, we worship him. David exhorted himself, "Bless the Lord, O my soul, and all that is within me, bless his holy name! Bless the Lord, O my soul, and forget not all his benefits" (Ps. 103:1–2).*
3. *Zion plays an important role in redemptive history, and the Psalms of Ascents reflect this significance. Retrace the references to Zion in Psalms 125:1; 126:1; 128:5; 129:5; 132:13; 133:3.*
4. *How will you respond differently this Lord's Day when your pastor pronounces the benediction?*

Endnotes

Ch. 1 Your blessed life now

1 For this insight I am indebted to John Piper, *What Jesus Demands from the World* (Wheaton, IL: Crossway, 2006), 94–96.

Ch. 2 God's victory over evil

1 Quoted in Charles H. Spurgeon, *The Treasury of David* (Rio, WI: AGES Software, 2000), 5:198.

2 Quoted in J. C. Ryle, *Five English Reformers* (London: Banner of Truth, 1960), 109.

3 Edith Schaeffer, *The Tapestry: The Life and Times of Francis and Edith Schaeffer* (Waco, TX: Word, 1981), 398–401.

Ch. 3 Out of the depths

1 Michael Wilcock, *The Message of the Psalms 73–150* (The Bible Speaks Today; Downers Grove, IL: InterVarsity Press, 2001), 238.

2 Albert Barnes, *Barnes' Notes on the Bible* (Rio, WI: AGES Software, 2000), 5:1936.

3 For these and other instances in Luther's spiritual pilgrimage, see Roland Bainton, Here *I Stand: A Life of Martin Luther* (Peabody, MA: Hendrickson, 1977; 2009 repr.).

4 The Latin phrase *De profundis* means "Out of the depths" and was Luther's way of describing Psalm 130. From Albert Barnes, *Barnes' Notes on the Bible* (Rio, WI: AGES Software, 2000), 5:1936. There is no indication that Luther associated the torches with the devil's presence. It seems that, after his recovery, he simply wanted to praise God for the gospel, and nothing so spites the devil as that.

Ch. 4 Stressed!

1 Time, June 6, 1983 cover story. Cited online in "America's #1 Health Problem," at The American Institute of Stress at http://www.stress.org/americas.htm (accessed July 18, 2011).

2 Statistics from a 1996 survey by the National Mental Health Association. Cited online at http://www.health.ri.gov/disease/diabetes/stress.php (accessed April 10, 2008).

3 "Stress: Physical Effects," May 12, 2007, at http://relaxation-stress-reduction.suite101.com/article.cfm/stress_physical_effects (accessed July 18, 2011).

4 Derek Kidner, *Psalms 73–150* (Tyndale Old Testament Commentary; London: InterVarsity Press, 1975), 448.

5 "Be Still, My Soul" at http://hymntime.com/tch/htm/b/e/s/bestill.htm (accessed February, 2012).

Ch. 5 Seeking God's presence

1 Stephen R. Covey, A. Roger Merrill, and Rebecca R. Merrill, *First Things First* (New York: Fireside, 1994), 88–89.

Ch. 6 Experiencing God's presence

1 Iain H. Murray, *Jonathan Edwards: A New Biography* (Edinburgh: Banner of Truth, 1987), 35–36.

Ch. 7 The beauty of unity

1 In R. Kent Hughes, *Philippians: The Fellowship of the Gospel—Preaching the Word* (Wheaton, IL: Crossway, 2007), 164.

Ch. 8 Blessing given and received

1 Hughes Oliphant Old, *Leading in Prayer: A Workbook for Ministers* (Grand Rapids: Eerdmans, 1995), 350.

Also available

This brief journey

Loving and Living the Psalms of Ascents (Vol. 1)

RHETT DODSON

128PP, PAPERBACK

ISBN 978-1-84625-354-6

The Psalms of Ascents were sung by Israelites as they made their way to Jerusalem for the annual feasts of Passover, Pentecost, and Tabernacles. As pilgrim songs, they provide a way for believers to express their fears, needs, and aspirations as they journey through this life. These psalms are also the songs of Jesus. In this book and its companion volume, To Be a Pilgrim, discover how these ancient songs of Israel affect your faith today, point you to the future, and help you keep your eyes on Christ every step of the way.

This is a great read of unusual quality for its clarity, shrewd insights, and practical, pastoral stimulus. The contemporary applications are down-to-earth and realistic, as well as challenging and motivational, heart-warming, and spirit-uplifting. This is the best sort of expository Bible teaching, which I commend both very warmly and very gratefully for the blessing it has been to me.
David Jackman, past President of the Proclamation Trust, London, UK, and author of *Teaching Isaiah*

In a day when expositions can polarize into either very dry bread or very mushy bread, here is a fine feast. In this book and its companion volume, Rhett Dodson expounds the wonderful "Psalms of Ascents" with attention to the text and its message, illustrations drawn from rich wells, familiarity with the normal Christian life, and readability that befits a good communicator.
Simon Manchester, Senior Minister, St. Thomas Anglican Church, North Sydney, Australia, and author of *Six Steps to Talking about Jesus*

Also available

In the care of the Good Shepherd

Meditations on Psalm 23

IAIN D CAMPBELL

112PP, PAPERBACK

ISBN 978-1-84625-175-7

There is probably no passage of Scripture with which people are more familiar than the twenty-third psalm. The words of the metrical version are among the best loved and most often sung of our Scottish Metrical Psalms. Every statement of the psalm is loaded with meaning and with significance and importance. Enjoy reading through these inspiring meditations on Psalm 23.

'Iain D. Campbell's exposition of Psalm 23 is masterful, both exegetically and pastorally. Reminiscent of the late Douglas MacMillan's work on this psalm, Dr Campbell's adds significantly to our appreciation of the psalm; indeed, under his guidance we are led to behold new vistas of greener pastures and still waters. Sure-footed expository genius of a rare kind.'

Derek Thomas, Reformed Theological Seminary, Jackson, Mississippi, USA

'The book is written by one who functions as an under-shepherd of the Saviour and who is aware of the spiritual needs and desires of his flock, and this experience is very much to the fore throughout the work. Further, the activities of Jesus are described in such a straightforward devotional manner that makes the book a joy to read. It is a book suitable for the heart as well as for the mind.'

Revd Dr Malcolm Maclean, Minister, Scalpay Free Church of Scotland

About Day One:

Day One's threefold commitment:

- To be faithful to the Bible, God's inerrant, infallible Word;
- To be relevant to our modern generation;
- To be excellent in our publication standards.

I continue to be thankful for the publications of Day One. They are biblical; they have sound theology; and they are relevant to the issues at hand. The material is condensed and manageable while, at the same time, being complete—a challenging balance to find. We are happy in our ministry to make use of these excellent publications.

JOHN MACARTHUR, PASTOR-TEACHER, GRACE COMMUNITY CHURCH, CALIFORNIA

It is a great encouragement to see Day One making such excellent progress. Their publications are always biblical, accessible and attractively produced, with no compromise on quality. Long may their progress continue and increase!

JOHN BLANCHARD, AUTHOR, EVANGELIST AND APOLOGIST